THE CC
ORDERING
SERVICE

101 Orders For Daily Use

Stephen Richards

THE COSMIC ORDERING SERVICE

101 Orders For Daily Use

First Edition
Published in Great Britain
by Mirage Publishing 2007

Text Copyright © Stephen Richards 2007

First published in paperback 2007

A CIP catalogue record for this book
Is available from the British Library.

ISBN 13: 978-1-90257-823-1
ISBN 10: 1902578236

Mirage Publishing
PO Box 161
Gateshead
NE8 4WW
Great Britain

Printed and bound in Great Britain by

Forward Press
Remus House, Coltsfoot Drive, Woodston,
Peterborough, PE2 9JX

Cover designed by Sharon Anderson, Artistic Director
Cover ©Mirage Publishing

For all my Cosmic Friends in difficulty

Contents

Introduction   11

1. Beat Insomnia   23
2. Beat Asthma, Hay Fever and Eczema 24
3. Beat Irritable Bowl Syndrome 25
4. Beat Worry   26
5. Beat Incontinence   27

6. Better at Helping Others   28
7. Better at Making a Decision 29
8. Better Car   30
9. Better Fitness and Health 31
10. Better Holidays   32
11. Better House   33
12. Better Job   34
13. Better Memory   35
14. Better Pain Control   36
15. Better Sex   37
16. Better Time Management 38
17. Better Wealth Creation 39

 A Word about Relationship Abuse 55
18. Conquer Destructive Abuse 56
19. Conquer Economic Abuse 57
20. Conquer Emotional Abuse 58
21. Conquer Humiliation Abuse 59
22. Conquer Intimidation Abuse 60
23. Conquer Isolation Abuse 61
24. Conquer Sexual Abuse 62
25. Conquer Stealth Abuse 63
26. Conquer Threat Abuse 64

27. Find a Soul Mate 65
28. Find Lesbian Love 66
29. Find Male Homosexual Love 67
30. Find Spiritual Awakening 68

31. Overcome Depression 69
32. Overcome Fears/Phobias 70
33. Overcome Guilt 71
34. Overcome Life's Pressure 72
35. Overcome Loneliness 73
36. Overcome Panic Attacks 74
37. Overcome Test Anxiety 75
38. Overcome Tiredness/Laziness 76

39. Successful Anger Control 77
40. Successful Dating 78
41. Successful Debt Management 79
42. Successful Ego-boost 80
43. Successful Home Improvements 81
44. Successful In Vitro (IVF) 82
45. Successful Internet Dating 83
46. Successful Speed Dating 84
47. Successful Sport Performance 85
48. Successful Weight Loss 86

A Word about Quitting Drugs 87
49. Quit Antidepressants 88
50. Quit Boozing 89
51. Quit Cocaine 90
52. Quit Ecstasy 91
53. Quit Gambling 92
54. Quit Hallucinogens 93
55. Quite Heroin 94
56. Quit Marijuana 95

57.	Quit Methamphetamine	96
58.	Quit Painkillers	97
59.	Quit Sleeping Pills	98
60.	Quit Smoking	99
61.	Quit Steroids	100
62.	Quit Sunbathing	101
63.	Quit Tranquillisers	102

Health

64.	Anti-Ageing	103
65.	Parenting Hyperactivity Disorder (ADHD)	104
66.	Cosmic Surgery	105
67.	Detox my Body	106
68.	Eating Disorders	107
69.	Female Infertility	109
70.	Health Creation	110
71.	Male Infertility	111
72.	Nightmare Control	112
73.	Obsessive-Compulsive Disorder	113
74.	Preparing for Surgery	114
75.	Skin & Body Care	115
76.	Terminal Illness	116

Miscellaneous

77.	Bereavement Recovery	117
78.	Bullying	118
79.	Chakra Maintenance	119
80.	Cosmic Ordering Hits a Brick Wall	125
81.	Debt Crisis	127
82.	Learning Ability	128
83.	Racism	129
84.	Save the World	130
85.	Transcending Challenges	133

Relationship & Sexual

86.	Addicted to Internet Porn, Cybersex	134
87.	Addicted to Sex	135
88.	Accepting Homosexuality	136
89.	Become a Latin Lover	137
90.	Cheating Partner	138
91.	Children Being Used Against a Partner	139
92.	Increase Sex Drive	140
93.	Love Rival in Your Way	141
94.	Obsessive Ex is Stalking Me	142
95.	Power and Control (overcoming)	143
96.	Relationship Breakdown	144
97.	Sexual Fantasy	145
98.	Wedding Day Bliss	146

Special Orders

99.	Attain Fame	147
100.	Immortality	148
101.	Slowing Time Down	149
	Cosmic Questions & Answers	151
	Other Titles	188

Introduction

This book has come about due to the many followers of Cosmic Ordering asking me for help in wording or tailoring Orders to suit their circumstances.

Although there are many success stories, there could be many more. Looking at the content of some of your questions directed at me, it would seem that life is full of problems that you want to be able to take care of.

Your problems are so varied, and for some it would seem that the more you try to solve them, the more that new problems occur.

I am regularly inundated with multiples of the same question, from many different Cosmic Friends. I say 'Friends' because I class ALL involved with Cosmic Ordering to be my Friends, with a capital 'F' to stress the importance of that friendship.

For many of you, Ordering wealth seems to be an easy task, but some of you are getting a little unstuck when it comes to the other Orders.

You can sweep problems under the carpet or run away from them. But wherever you go, sooner or later, there will be problems for you to solve.

Many of you will have already developed skills in handling problems in life, but Cosmic Ordering can and does expedite problematic situations swiftly to the recycle bin. I want to empower you and give you some insights on how to deal with problems in life so that you may achieve success and happiness.

Before you commence with Cosmic Ordering, one of the best ways to proceed is to have the right attitude towards what you want. Of course, having the right attitude but using it with a poor Cosmic Ordering discipline does not mix very well.

The Cosmic Ordering Service

You are reading this because you have hit a brick wall when it comes to successfully Ordering what you want, but sometimes problems may be blessings in disguise.

You see, problems may be the Cosmos' way of trying to assist us in creating opportunities for us to grow and become better human beings. I don't mean that some entity is watching out for us and deliberately putting obstacles in our way just so that it can show us an opportunity.

Should a problem come along then it does not mean it is the end of the dream: you can turn it to your advantage. That is what I mean by assistance; assistance in turning a problem into a profit-making opportunity…in more ways than one!

This is a difficult situation, because your particular problem(s) may be hiding an opportunity that not only creates personal growth but also creates wealth and success in abundance.

Without doubt, there should be a solution to every problem. You have to look at it in an oblique sort of way, and here's why. A problem without a solution is not a problem.

Modern-day transport has come about as a result of the problem of getting from A to B in a fast way.

Looking at it this way, a problem can actually be motivational! You might have a problem that means you join a group, with many sharing the same problem. I do not want to single out any specific group, as this would be unfair and look like I was picking on that one particular thing, but you get what I mean.

What can happen is that you will meet new friends that will bring you into a better life than the life you were living previously.

Sometimes a problem can easily be overcome, and without the need for applying Cosmic Ordering to the situation, so please think about the problem before applying yourself to making that Cosmic Connection.

Just out of interest, I am guessing that you are familiar with the principles of Cosmic Ordering, yes? However, should you have picked this book up just because of the pretty picture on the front cover, hopped on a train or plane and thought that by having this book that this is all you have to do in order to know everything there is to know about Cosmic Ordering, then you are in for a long ride!

This is not the place for me to start teaching you about making the connection. By virtue of you picking this book up and reading it, you should already be familiar with the basic ideology behind Cosmic Ordering and the naturalistic means of connecting to the Cosmos.

Sorry if this seems like I am patronising you, but I would only be antagonising my Cosmic Friends who already know about the basic principles of connecting to the Cosmos if I were to try and cover that subject again within these limited amount of pages. Space is precious, so I do not want to go over old ground.

Also, if you are sceptical about Cosmic Ordering, I make no apology for asking you to stop wasting your time in reading any further, as I am only concerned with helping the genuine believer in Cosmic Ordering. I am not interested in converting non-believers, as this is not a religion or some cult that needs disingenuine followers with a half-hearted belief, as it only serves to gives negative feedback to interested parties who may have otherwise wished to explore Cosmic Ordering.

If you are a complete newcomer to Cosmic Ordering, I would also ask you to stop reading any further, as you are wasting your time, and I do not want to be blamed for that. For an in-depth coverage of Cosmic Ordering, I would suggest that you first read my book 'Cosmic Ordering Guide: Where Dreams can become Reality'. Sorry to harp on, but I really do care about you, I really want you to gain all what you can from your life, as life is so, so precious.

I make no apologies for helping you gain what you want out of life. My own life was a living hell, I have been there myself. I remember waiting for my state handouts to be delivered through my letterbox by the postman, only to find the postman/woman walking on by without stopping to put my welfare cheque (in the UK we call it Jobseekers Allowance) through the door.

The worse thing was, it was a Saturday morning, there would be no more mail until the following Monday! How my stomach would growl over that weekend! By the time Monday arrived I was a wreck

No-one can tell you that you do not deserve some extras in your life, and why shouldn't you have a better car, house, career, relationship, bank balance, holiday, health, education and the likes? This is what Cosmic Ordering is all about, and then thereafter you can go for the spiritual stages. You have to experience what it is like to have material pleasures to be able to see what lies beyond them. Without this experience you may always long for those material things you never had, but always coveted.

Get me, I sound like a right spiritual guru! I am not advocating anything spiritual or that you follow some spiritual path. Far from it. I want you to experience the pleasures of a materialistic world, I want you to have this in abundance, as only then can you know what I am talking about now.

You have to believe to receive. Problems are a learning experience. Unless a problem occurs, you will not learn why something happens the way it does. You cannot change your viewpoints and opinions unless you have a first-hand experience of problems.

Problems can cause you to become active in helping others. This is how many self-help organisations first started out. Someone experienced a problem, they made it known that they would help others and then wham! A new organisation is born. People will pay a lot of money for help with problem-solving. Any company that introduces a new product will hire people to report the problems they find, and then the company refines the product until it's right.

One important point for you to digest, is never try to cover up a problem. Admit you have problems! What's the point of putting on a false smile and trying to make people think you are problem-free? It will only eat you away...inside out!

When you solve a problem that most people try to avoid or can't solve, you get recognition and their admiration. You may become a hero or heroine.

They (problems) also give you the chance to invent new ways of doing something, new ways that will save you time and make you happier with your life.

You can have the admiration of all those people who encountered the same problems but didn't do anything to solve them.

You also will find that when you look at problems with a POSITIVE mind, you will accomplish more, relieve stress and succeed.

Just think of some of the everyday issues that you have tried to make better via an Order: violence, drugs, suicide, gangs, teen subcultures, home invasions,

15

dishonesty, lawlessness, fear. All these things that you are uncomfortable about can be worth far more than money if they can be rectified.

Sometimes it is the negative characteristics of your community that you want to change. Such social problems worry almost every one of us but, until now, no one knew what to do about them. Only a minority of the population participates in such things. Yet that small minority upsets almost everyone to some degree.

Social problems will not decrease by themselves. Think about how much simpler and safer your life seemed to be 10 years ago, or 20 years ago. This book will turn around the belief that the situation is hopeless and provide a process to improve the quality of life for you and everyone else.

I know from the many communiqués I get from my Friends that they have lost faith in what they once depended on: police, courts, tribunals, politicians and disciplinarians in the education system to act against anti-social behaviour. The health sector is the supposed jewel in the crown, yet why are so many up in arms over medical neglect? Education was once a free right of everyone in the UK, yet look at the debts our students carry with them through their lives, all as a direct consequence of going to university. The problems get worse. So there are far more pressing cases than just asking the Cosmos for a cash windfall.

We used to trust people in our communities. Now we don't know if we can trust our neighbours.

It was only two generations ago that TV, billboard, racing circuits, snooker sponsorship and cinema commercials advertised that cigarette smoking was good for you, that it made you sophisticated, successful, popular. Now that belief has changed. We are left with a nation of nicotine addicts wanting to kick the habit. They want to do that more than land a parcel of cash...and that is something Cosmic Ordering can help with.

At the same time, consuming alcohol in large quantities was considered a challenge of the macho brigade, a way of life for the winners, the upwardly mobile, and the successful. Many have asked about how to obtain Cosmic help in kicking the alcohol habit.

Personal habits such as smoking and drinking can be curbed significantly, all with the correct 'clean' language used in your Order.

Those other things that disturb us so much can also be changed too. This book will remove the huge burdens from each of you by showing you how to use 'clean' language in placing your Order.

For those with children, it is about what they want for their futures: better health, education, careers and home lives and how they can be taught to cope with its ups and downs.

Meanwhile, we also want to make improvements that will begin to take effect within our lifetimes.

You don't have to be a university scholar or a politician to say what you mean, what you stand for, what you believe is good and right.

You will likely find your situation in here. You will see how much we all have in common. Most of us have serious concerns about the world we live in. In some cases, fear and worry play a significant role in our lives. Conditions in our communities seem so much beyond our understanding that they seem to be out of control. Changes could make the quality of our lives better. We want change, but feel helpless to control it.

Helplessness is a perception, a widespread belief. But it is not reality. We look for short-term solutions rather than long-term cures. Something can be done.

This book will illuminate the path that can be followed. We will consider what can be done, the objectives, goals and steps in the process toward improvement.

Most of us know at least one person whose life has been profoundly affected by something violent, something invasive, something that changed that person's life forever. Personal violence is a problem that upsets many of us deeply. Lately, even invasion of privacy by computer hackers has risen as a form of personal psychological violence.

Cosmic Ordering can be used to abate your fears; once you have made your connection, then you can run your Order through your mind, by naturalistic means. Hear yourself say the words, as per the Order that applies to your situation. I am sure you can find one within this book that fits your need.

I am not saying that you should tailor any particular Order just for the sake of it: if you do not find what you are looking for, find an Order that is as close to your situation as you can, then start using the positives from it and apply them to your own Order.

Clean language is the key to making it work for you. For instance, don't fall into the trap of saying, 'My life is *rubbish*, I *can't* make things happen. *Nothing* good happens to me, always the *bad* things of life come my way. I want to change all of that, please help me make those things happen.'

Look at the negative words (highlighted in the Order in italics) used in that Order:

- Rubbish
- Can't
- Nothing
- Bad

Rephrased, replacing negative words with positive words (in italics), as follows: 'My life is becoming *better*. I *can* have *good* things happen. The *good* things of life *come my way*. I *want* to *allow* that to *continue* to happen, as appropriate. Please make those things happen from now onwards.'

Some of the neutral words I have listed below are in the grey area, so use as appropriate to your situation:

- Make
- Happen
- Please

Let me rephrase the following with some neutrals removed or made more positive: 'My life is rubbish, I can't make things happen. Nothing good happens to me, always the bad things of life come my way. I want to change all of that, please help me make those things happen.'

Revised Order using positive words (in italics), as follows: 'Day by day, my life is *improving. Good* things happen. *Good* things come my way. *Allow* that to *continue*, as appropriate. I can *continue* making those things *happen.*'

Note the phrase: *continue* making those things *happen.* See how it actually gives an Order within the Order. You will find plenty of that in the 101 Orders within this book. Look out for them and incorporate such phraseology into your own Order(s).

I am sure you get the idea, and I am sure you could improve the way you phrase your Order(s) by use of clean language. With a little bit of practice, you will soon be using clean language in everyday conversation, as well as your Orders.

If you do not use clean language in the Order, the negative words can be literally taken as part of the Order, and then you wonder why your Order has gone adrift, or only partly manifested.

Just out of interest, I have not used clean language in this introduction, so please do not berate me. Perhaps if I used clean language then it might look like this:

START
You can have good happen to you when using clean language. This is the best way to enhance the good that you are already experiencing.
END

See if you can pick out the neutrals, can you improve on them? Don't go rushing for a pen, this is not that sort of book. I want you to have an easy time of it, as you deserve it.

When placing an Order, address the Cosmos with respect. I am not going to append this salutation before every Order within this book, but please do so with your own Order. Start something like, 'Oh, Mighty Cosmos', or even 'Dear Cosmos'.

During the course of the Order, ensure you clearly mark out your path, as it is often a case that the Order can be misconstrued, for example 'Oh, Mighty Cosmos, I have some lovely shoes, they are nice. How I would like some more'.

Yes, you could get more...lots more! So DO mark out in a clear and concise way, how may pairs of shoes you want! Like so, 'Oh, Mighty Cosmos, I have some lovely shoes (give the size, colour, etc), they are nice. I want another pair that are, as appropriate, equally nice'.

When ending your Order, always leave the Cosmos on a positive note. Something along the lines of, 'I leave you with this in peace, thank you'.

Sometimes there is a need to use a negative value in your Order. What I mean by this is, in order to take something away from you that might be causing harm, it is necessary to add a negative word that you might not wish to use. For instance, 'The stimulation I get from the ultraviolet rays from the Sun that release chemicals in me produce a natural high, but I now ask that I get an even more natural high within me *without* the Sun.'

The word inserted into this Order is 'without', as it relates to getting along *without* the Sun. By using the phrase 'without the Sun', it reinforces your lack of need for the Sun. So do use these negatives to your advantage and where needed, as they will actually help.

You will see some of this set out in the Orders I have worked on within the book. Do try to incorporate them into your Orders.

Make your Order concise and precise as possible. Don't ramble on needlessly.

This is not a book of 'affirmations', as that falls to a different discipline, although you can certainly use affirmations throughout the day, as they do reinforce certain things.

You will find the Orders do contain some affirmations: these are to reinforce the Order, but are not

21

meant to be solely accepted as affirmations to replace those you might ordinarily use throughout the day. However, I do not use any affirmations for myself. This might surprise some of you, but I have, to some degree, transcended the need for self support in this area. I can now draw directly from the Cosmos, as I know you will eventually transcend to.

You will find the Order relating to the specific situation beneath the short write-up. As short as some of them are, that is all that is required. However, do add specifics where necessary.

Best wishes ever,

Steve r

Beat Insomnia

Most adults have experienced insomnia or sleeplessness at one time or another in their lives. Although most of us know what insomnia is and how we feel and perform after one or more sleepless nights, few seek medical advice. Many people remain unaware of the behavioural and medical options available to treat insomnia. Insomnia affects all age groups. Among older adults, insomnia affects women more often than men. The incidence increases with age.

Certain groups are at higher risk of developing insomnia: the aged, pregnant women, shift workers, women in menopause, people in chronic pain, adolescents or young students.

Common stimulants associated with poor sleep include caffeine and nicotine. You should consider not only restricting caffeine use in the hours immediately before bedtime but also limiting your total daily intake. Alcohol is associated with sleep disruption and creates a sense of non-refreshed sleep in the morning.

"I want to regain control over my coordination, memory focus and concentration. Let my healing thoughts automatically and instinctively heal any medical or psychological cause of insomnia within me.

"I remain alert throughout the day and expend energy in abundance on the things I do. I want to be free of anxiety and any hidden depression.

"I find my bedroom to be a comfortable place where I can relax, even more than I have done before. I want to focus on any underlying condition and improve my sleeping patterns. Let the melatonin that is secreted by my pineal gland be the right amount needed for me."

Beat Asthma, Hay Fever and Eczema

The mystery of why farm children have far fewer allergies may have been solved. For years scientists have speculated that something in the rural environment protects against allergies such as hay fever, asthma and eczema, with some research showing the risk is half that of someone living in a city. But exactly what is responsible for such an effect has not been tracked down.

Scientists have discovered that the answer lies in the cowshed and, in particular, in two strains of bacteria: Acinetobacter lwoffiiand and Lactococcus lactis.

When they made the bacteria into nose drops and gave them to laboratory animals, they were immediately protected from allergies. Now the aim is to develop a human version of the drops, which could be the first preventive treatment for the growing problem of allergies. This supports the hair of the dog theory: that which gives to you can take it away. In the meantime, try this Order.

"My immune system is to become desensitised, as appropriate, to everyday things such as pollen, dust and to certain foods. (Not for those with nut allergies.)

"I want my health immune system to have accelerated learning and false memory of exposure to early life bacteria, infections and other potential problems, and to use these memories as tools to fight asthma, hay fever and eczema. Let this 'memory' exposure help to calibrate my once naive immune system.

"I want low levels of allergy, hay fever, asthma and/or eczema (delete whichever does not apply to you). I will increase my intake of fresh fruit and raw vegetables, allow these to increase my resistance."

Beat Irritable Bowl Syndrome

Doctors are not sure what causes IBS. The nerves and muscles in the bowel appear to be extra sensitive in people with IBS. Muscles may contract too much when you eat. These contractions can cause cramping and diarrhea during or shortly after a meal. Or the nerves may react when the bowel stretches, causing cramping or pain.

I have personal experience of this, as when I was in a hurry or experienced some sort of physical interference, like my phone ringing, etc, my stomach used to be lifted by the muscles contracting beneath it. I would often feel like throwing the food up, which I suppose is different to most IBS symptoms. Anyway, I overcame it with an Order.

"I want to regain control over how my large intestine and digestive system works. I want to avoid fatty foodstuffs and carbonated drinks. Let me instinctively know if I need to increase fibre intake in the form of healthy cereals. The food I eat is to be instinctively selected so as I do not produce digestive gasses.

"I am good at planning meals, let that planning allow for smaller meals on a more regular basis throughout the day. I want the food I eat to be able to pass through my digestive system in a normal and healthy way.

"Allow a more comfortable feeling in my abdomen when I eat. Diarrhoea or constipation is a thing of the past. I will now pass normal stools. Emotionally, I want to be stress free, which in turn will lessen cramping.

"I want to find it easier to manage my symptoms, I can do this exercising more and increasing my fresh water intake, as appropriate."

Beat Worry

In a difficult world, fear and worry are two of our biggest problems. You are not alone. Many share them.

Often we don't face up to what we fear. We try to hide it in the bottom of our minds, so that perhaps we don't even know what we are afraid of, or are worrying about. It is important to find out exactly what we are afraid of, and also try to understand how the fear started. There may be a particular time, or event, which started it off.

Fear comes in many forms: what the future holds, bad luck, death, lack of money, lack of love, failure, being all alone, other people.

"Give me the strength to banish worry from my life. As each day passes make me stronger. Let me find someone I can trust, and share how I feel.

"My character is a strong one, it can cope even more as time goes on. I want to learn to think in positive ways. Let my new mind think differently, as appropriate. I will become more caring about myself in what I eat and in how much rest I take.

"I want to find new surroundings that are conducive to my new and positive thoughts. I want to get more involved in things that are a benefit to other people. I can feel control of my emotions returning to me in a strong way, I feel that now and want it to happen.

"I can postpone worrying until a later date when I am worry-free, let me enjoy myself until then. I am allowed to be happy and positive, all else is postponed indefinitely.

"I want to learn to let go and to lift both feet off the proverbial ground, as appropriate. I deserve a break from it all, now I want to concentrate on my needs and being happy within myself."

Beat Incontinence

This often-kept secret, which causes humiliation, isolation, depression and fear, is known as incontinence: the unexpected and unwanted leaking of urine from the bladder. It's time we brought this disabling subject out of the water closet and into the open.

Urinary incontinence does not just afflict the elderly. It can happen at any age and can be caused by a variety of conditions, some temporary, some permanent.

Temporary causes of incontinence are urinary tract infection, vaginal infection, constipation, side effects from certain medicines, drinking alcohol or caffeine, using diuretics (water pills) and ingesting some foods such as chocolate.

A more permanent cause is a weakness of the muscles holding the bladder in place which occurs after childbirth. The bladder itself, or sphincter muscles, may be weak. Overactive bladder muscles, enlarged prostate, hormone imbalance in women, neurological disorders and immobility also can be contributing causes. I hope this Order will help

"I want to regain control over normal bladder function. I want to control when my bladder contracts so as to initiate the act of urinating. Let my bladder have a stable function and to seek permission from me before urinating, as appropriate.

"Allow my bladder to become more stable in holding fluid, let the shut-off valve work efficiently under my control of opening and shutting off as and when I want.

"When my bladder is full let me avoid the situations that can cause urination. I want to have fluid intake as normal, and to control when I urinate."

27

Better at Helping Others

All the time, every moment of the day, we're in the world and either making it better or making it worse. Because we're all inter-connected, our thoughts spread out and affect everything around us. When we feel bad, we might treat people in an ill-natured or thoughtless way, which can lower their mood, and they might do the same to the next person they meet, and so it carries on. So let's start and spread a bit of good.

There is a physics theory called 'The Butterfly Effect'. It goes like this: a butterfly flapping its wings in one part of the world can begin a chain of events in the air around it that causes a hurricane somewhere else on the planet. As that is so, I also believe that a single smile or a helping gesture can reverberate around the planet and possibly prevent a war or outbreak of violence in some far-off land. Just as an avalanche must begin with a single grain of snow, that one grain had to be the first.

I would like to thank my Cosmic Friend, Mervyn of Creative Counselling in Belfast, for recommending this Order (*www.creativecounselling.org*).

"Let me be a tool of the Cosmos, allow me to engage with this positive energy to develop awareness and bring well-being to myself and others. I want to penetrate into the essence of all being and significance, and to release the power of that inner attainment for the guidance and benefit of others. As we are created from love and light, let that birthright shine on all. Let my positive transmission of energy radiate out to those I wish to help. The electromagnetic force gained through my pineal gland enables me to bond with the Universe, let that be used for the good of all. Let that happen from now onwards."

Better at Making a Decision

We all make decisions of varying importance every day, so the idea that decision-making can be a rather sophisticated art may at first seem strange. However, studies have shown that most people are much poorer at decision making than they think.

Good decision-making is an essential skill for career success generally, and effective leadership particularly. If you can learn to make timely and well-considered decisions, then you can often lead your team to spectacular and well-deserved success.

When the decision we are facing is a life changing one is it any wonder we stop in our tracks? Let's see if this Order will get things moving for you.

"I am already good at making decisions, I am able to decide where I park my car, what time I have to set off for a meeting and when to go to bed, allow that decision-making principle to be invoked in what I have to decide upon, which is (describe it).

"I only want to work on the information available, putting aside emotive interests. Let selective use of the information at hand occur in an instinctive way. Allow the quantity of information that can be processed by my mind be limited to the decision.

"There is a stream of decisions surrounding this decision, many decisions made earlier have led up to this decision and make it possible to be concluded one way or the other, allow that to happen now.

"Already a decision has been made, the Universe has made the answer available to me from the many alternatives available. I now know what my decision is."

Better Car

You don't like the thought of extra payments every month for a new car so you put up with the wreck you are driving. Perhaps someone you have fallen out with bought the car for you and you want to lose the memory.

You want a car with better fuel economy, but are unwilling to sacrifice size or performance to get it. You want a practical alternative that is actually better for the environment. Get the smallest, most efficient vehicle that makes sense for your daily driving.

It's a common dilemma: to lease or buy a car - which is better? Everyone who has ever considered leasing has had this question cross their mind.

"I want a safer, more ergonomically comfortable and fuel efficient car. It must be as good as any reasonable person would expect. Let the mileage be correct. Any history about its past should be true. Let the ride of the car be exceptional and the colour to be one of my choice.

"Let the safety and durability of the car I want be of paramount importance. It must do what I'd reasonably expect of a car of its size, price and type. It should also do whatever the seller promises. Let the car correspond in every detail with any advert I saw for it, and anything the salesman says about it. If I am promised a new car, it should arrive perfect and unused.

"Let me find the means to purchase the car, ensure that I obtain extra income from working (etc), let my ability to earn more income increase. Let my earned income meet my desire for a new/replacement car. Let the creative part of my mind create new ideas to earn extra money."

30

Better Fitness and Health

Sit in a quiet place. Think of your fitness goals. Now, close your eyes and imagine looking in the mirror and seeing a fit and younger looking you. Imagine feeling full of energy, free of illness, and more fun-loving throughout the day.

You should try to get outside, move around more often if you want to gain good health. Get in the open, outdoors and do some adventurous things that will help you with your diet. You can do anything from hiking to playing volleyball. This is exactly the way to get your body moving and keep the weight off, and at the same time make yourself fit. You do not have to over exert yourself, just so long as you keep your body in motion.

Try cycling for fitness. Cycling is a great way to lose weight. You can help take off those unwanted pounds by riding your bike. You can take bike rides around town or on a trail near by. No matter where you go, you will have a great ride and see new things and you will find great pleasure in exercising.

"I want to drink more water, as appropriate, and to allow it to help remove metabolic wastes. Let it provide me with more energy for my activities.

"The more I exercise the more I want to rev up my metabolism to allow for quicker, natural fat loss. Keep my mind sharp, and provide consistent energy throughout the day. Teach me to eat till I am satisfied and not overfull so that I get hungry again for the next small meal. Raw foods are live foods and give us energy. I seek healthier habits and tasty alternatives that will fit my lifestyle.

"Maintain my heart rate at a healthy level when strength training, resistance or weight training."

Better Holidays

Would you be surprised to learn that two-thirds of all British people have their holidays in July and August? The traditional seaside holiday is not quite as popular as it was, but people still flock to the more traditional haunts of Blackpool, Brighton and Scarborough. Of course, there's nothing worse than spending a wet weekend stuck in a guesthouse with your children (partner, etc) desperate for some seaside fun.

With package holidays becoming more popular and within the reach of most, it's not surprising that Brits are flocking abroad more often. Wouldn't you like to go to the Caribbean, or maybe to the island of Phuket, in Thailand, for a truly memorable holiday?

The most popular destination for Brits is Spain, followed by France. The most popular method of travel is plane, followed by sea, then the Channel Tunnel.

"I want to go to a holiday destination that suits me (my family, etc). The holiday will be the best I have been on and one of the most affordable, as I want to earn more (salary, bonus, etc) so I can feel the benefit of the work I have applied to make the money. I would like a situation to happen that will give me the opportunity of making more money for spending on the holiday.

"Let everyone in my group/family be able to take that holiday and to be given the protection of the Divine Light. Focus and attention will be paid to the fine details of the holiday itinerary so that all in my group are catered for.

"I am carefree and can let go of stress, make that even more possible when I am on holiday. Create an ambience on holiday that is memorable for the fun times. Allow my high spirits to enthuse all in my group (or yourself)."

Better House

Fancy a move to a better house, invariably in a high demand area! It is no use just putting that Order to the Cosmos, as you actually have to create the means to how it will come about. What if you want that smart semi-detached house with built-on garage but don't have the money? Some would give up hope in an instance. I have personal experience of a number of my Cosmic Friends actually securing better houses without the actual means to buy them at the time they placed their Order!

Also, with the global warming threat, many people who want to live in an ecological house think they can't afford it. They see expensive solar systems on the roof, bafflingly complex heating and hot water devices, and unusual, custom architecture. Now that ecological or 'sustainable' architecture is becoming trendy, they see high price tags for the 'added' sustainable features.

"I and my family are worthy of better accommodation, and in a better area. I ask that the house of my dreams will come about by virtue of my ability to make extra income. That extra income will come about with an increased sense of self-worth in myself. I am a valuable asset to society, my skills are a gift of life and will become more sought after and will be rewarded accordingly.

"Reserve that house for my family and I, make me a big house with plenty of rooms and beautiful to look at. It will be everything I dreamed it to be, the decoration is as I like it, the neighbours will be nice, kind people and I will feel it is my property by right. I will soon be able to sell/move from the house I am in and into my new luxury home."

Better Job

We often define ourselves by what we do – 'Hi, I'm Jim, and I'm a bank manager'. It's no mystery then that losing your job or changing occupations ranks as one of the most stressful transitions in life. In our hopscotch culture, bouncing from career to career is common, but the effects are no less difficult: making new friends, learning new tasks, living within a new budget and embracing a new identity.

Somewhere at around 30-35 years of age the hype wears off if there is no intuitive talent to keep the career advancing. Slow promotions, loss of challenge, major mistakes or accidents increase. A job will go from bad to worse if the core duties do not match our innate talents. Natural talents are the heart of career satisfaction and ultimate success; and each of us has enough for more than one career. Let's see if we can get your career moving.

"Let me know the difference between my learned skills, my motivation and my innate skills. I want to find the really ideal career, it should represent something I am motivated to pursue (your interests and your values). The ideal career I want should represent my innate skills, my talents. It is my talents that intuitively will understand the job and seek to grow.

"I want to select a new career because it fits my worth and education or past work experience (learned skills), they will provide for a best fit. I will instinctively know what a good fit job looks like, it will be my perfect career, and it is already earmarked for me. Busy people will take their time to meet with me, they will sense that I am serious and will listen to me."

Better Memory

Memory is the process of registering, consolidating, storing, and recalling information and also is the result of that process.

Memory is an electrochemical process of the brain and nervous system in which specialised brain centres receive, consolidate, store, and respond to new information.

The more memory traces you amass from sensory experiences, thoughts, feelings, and actions, the more ways you have to recall a particular piece of information.

A stimulating environment makes a major contribution to improving your memory. New information becomes a memory by moving from sensory memory to short-term memory. There, working memory creates the connections to consolidate it into long-term memory. Memory contains two kinds of material: knowledge - both general and personal - and procedures. Procedures do not require conscious attention in order to function.

"I want to invoke my natural abilities to maintain and improve my memory. Allow my sensory awareness to collect information in a super-fast way from my senses and to amass the memory traces so I can remember people, places, and events. Enhance my mental imaging ability so I can visualise an image of something or someone I want to remember. I want the words used to help me remember in a number of ways, including verbal memory traces. Allow me to use acronyms, rhymes, or jingles to help jog my memory. Making new connections is the process which relates new information to what I already know, thereby making the new information easier to recall."

Better Pain Control

In this section, I refer to pain that is caused by anything other than terminal illness (do not use if terminally ill).

Pain does not result just from physical disorders, but also from combinations of physiological, pathological, emotional, psychological, cognitive, environmental, and social factors.

When pain is experienced, this sensation has reached the cerebrum through complex and dynamic interactions. Heat on the skin, for example, results in chemical and electrical signals being sent through peripheral sensory nerves to the dorsal horn of the spinal cord. Whether this stimulus becomes painful depends on many factors.

When the stimulus becomes unpleasant the normal responses are to recognise the sensation as pain, to withdraw, and to avoid the activity. These responses can be expressed as sensory, motor, cognitive, motivational, and attentional consequences of the stimulus.

"I want successful pain control over the mechanisms within me. When pain is initiated and maintained I want physical and psychosocial interventions to alleviate it, as appropriate. I want to continue to experience the sense of touch and to receive signals that tell me of how my health is. From now on I want to generate a fundamental change in attitude and expectation about such control. I also want to exert such pain control by using preventive and active strategies, including physical and psychosocial interventions.

"Allow my higher centres to block or enhance the message wholly or partly through behavioural, cognitive activities."

Better Sex

Women do not separate sex from the emotional aspects of the relationship. They want a sense of connection and intimacy that starts well before sex is initiated.

Men often view making love as a primary way to connect with their mates. Men are more prone to visual stimulation and instant gratification.

Many couples find sex most enjoyable when they both know what to expect. Predictability can be either positive or negative. If you find you have a sexual routine but both you and your spouse satisfy each other's needs consistently, then it's positive. However, routine sex habits can be negative if they keep you from exploring new ways to satisfy each other.

"I want to sexually communicate with my partner as a couple, and may find out my partner would like to try something new that we both feel comfortable with.

"Adding spice to my love life by experimenting with the frequency, duration or time of day I have sex, or by adding foreplay or using sex toys.

"I want to challenge personal beliefs, and for my partner and I to become comfortable with our bodies and desires, and to consider stepping out of our comfort zones to fully enjoy all the possible sexual gratification and intimacy our relationship has to offer.

"Let us begin with open communication, each should ask what the other desires, and explore these desires together. Increase my libido high enough to encourage me to initiate sexual intercourse. My powers of seduction let me use foreplay as an enjoyable and satisfying experience for both my partner and me. Sexual activity can last as long as I want, and I can reach orgasm and climax."

37

Better Time Management

Many people spend their days in a frenzy of activity, but achieve very little because they are not concentrating on the right things.

If you've found yourself putting off important tasks over and over again, you're not alone. In fact, many people procrastinate to some degree - but some are so chronically affected by procrastination that it stops them achieving the things they're capable of and disrupts their careers.

In a nutshell, you procrastinate when you put off things that you should be focusing on right now, usually in favour of doing something that is more enjoyable or that you're more comfortable doing. Unfortunately, the big task isn't going to go away - truly important tasks rarely do.

"I want to make sure I know my priorities in life in order of importance. Let me leave the low-priority tasks to a more convenient time, concentring on the more important first. Important tasks asked of me will be attended to, allow me to do this to the exclusion of everything else, as appropriate. Let me overcome reluctance to get started.

"I want to find new ways of motivating myself to get moving on a task. Let me accept others checking up on me, so as to motivate me more. I now want to start being value for money to my employer/partner/friend (etc).

"Let me conquer procrastination and empower me to spot when I am doing it. I can overcome the block. I have good organisational and personal effectiveness habits, let these habits happen instinctively. I want to establish the right priorities, and manage my time in such a way that I can make the most of the opportunities open to me."

Better Wealth Creation

What was that religious phrase…*It is easier for a camel to go through the eye of a needle, than for a rich man to enter into…*

Well, it is easier for you to pass through the eye of a needle than it is for you to Cosmically Order wealth to land on your doorstep. This is a common misconception many of my Cosmic Friends are under. I reiterate: you cannot place an Order for that bag of money to be thrown at you from a rich philanthropist who just happens to be passing by. For those of you not familiar with my book, 'Cosmic Ordering Guide: Where Dreams Can Become Reality', I will reiterate what I say about gaining wealth: go for it piece by piece. That is how I achieved my wealth.

However, I must admit, I too became quite angry when that 'bag of money' never landed at my feet. It took me a little while to fathom it all out. Once I did, well, it all fell into place. That is when the money started rolling in by the bucket load. I did not get rich by writing books, I was wealthy long before I started writing, so do not attribute my book sales to how I am so wealthy now.

I am going to use an email reply I sent to one of my Cosmic Friends to show you how to attain wealth: it's a bit long, but worth it. The email is in the form of an answer to my Cosmic Friend complaining that their Order for money has not manifested. Here goes.

You say that you've got some sort of a block with your Order: no doubt a windfall/lottery win, etc. Well, you say you've wished for all of these regularly, but still nothing!

I can tell you that I am not surprised that you are not getting what you long for. I can tell you exactly what you are doing wrong, you are asking for the horse to be put before the cart! You want money/the lottery, etc to put this and that right, but you are not asking for the means to how the money or change in circumstance will come about. You are not a magician and cannot magic money to appear, just like that. I mean, have you bought 14,000,000 lottery tickets? You see, my Friend, just about everyone places an Order to win the lottery, this is why it is best to steer clear of that Order.

Why is it that I feel like giving the Cosmos a kick? We Order, we wait...and nothing happens! Damn!!! Double damn!!!

Not fully knowing your circumstances, I am going to take a decision here, a decision that makes me come to the conclusion that you either have a deep-seated negativity towards believing what will happen, and are therefore blocking your Order, or you have some deep-seated trouble from your current business life, which I suppose is obvious.

When did you last cleanse your chakras? Please, don't answer...I bet you have never done this! Anyway, that is what I suggest you do first. Stop using Cosmic Ordering.

The other matter is, you say that you have wished for all of these things regularly, or so it would seem from your email. You will know from having read my book that placing your Order once is enough, and then to put strategically placed reminders of what you want around your home. Like, for instance, put that giant awaited sale board on the fridge...if it will fit. If you really do want to go along the lottery route, then put your lottery ticket on the bathroom mirror where you can see it every day, buy it four weeks in advance and keep it there for that time, unless you win in the first week. So are you actually doing any of what I advise in my book?

Hmm, maybe not! So can you see where I am coming from?

Once you have cleansed your chakras and feel up to it, this is the time to go back to Cosmic Ordering. However, there is one set of circumstances when you can continually ask for the same thing, and this is via my 'Cosmic Ordering Connection' CD, which has been designed so you can ask as many times as you want for your Order. However, I do advise that you give Cosmic Ordering a break for a short while. Until you cleanse those chakras, don't ask at all for any Orders.

You covertly ask about asking for money. Most certainly, cash is a commodity, but how does that cash come about? That is what I mean by not asking for cash, it is better to ask for the means to have cash coming into your possession.

Think about it, cash is not going to land on your doorstep, but cash can come to you via increased earnings, selling something, winning something, etc. That is the way to go about making such a request, and it becomes more possible.

Ordering at night...it makes a great deal of difference. Have you ever tried to access your email account and found that the system is really slow to open, and then a little window pops up and tells you that the system is busy and to 'try again later'?

Although the sun never sets all over the world at the same time, you can be assured of it setting where you live. People turn off and go to bed, thus leaving you free to place an Order in a less busy zone, and the power of the moon assists in drawing your Order to you, mad as it sounds. It is all to do with electromagnetic energy.

You see, my Friend, some people just enter into Ordering in a willy-nilly fashion, they place their Order and think that's it! Well, it's not! Then they go back to Ordering only when it is a time of need, like now, and they have to try and recall how they made their first Order and find themselves in a muddle.

Imagine placing a different Order every day. It would eventually be like falling off a log, and not used just in times of hardship or emergency, when your mind cannot fully focus due to the dilemma you are in.

Remember this - if you make money your god, it will plague you like the devil.

Far too often, spiritually minded people throw up their hands and surrender to the lack of money syndrome. They have been conditioned to think that poverty is a fantastic learning experience, a kind of cleansing experience akin to being the Dalai Lama. They festoon themselves with imaginary banners proclaiming how it did wonders for the soul. To that I say: 'X+@#!' (You can imagine whichever expletive you wish.)

To pot with everything else, you have a birthright to exist in a state of wealth, health and happiness, in whichever order you want. And yet, some people dig themselves into a hellhole, and the hole gets deeper and deeper. After a while, that hole becomes a safe, familiar place to be. Of course, the problem with being stuck in a hole is that it is hard to see the sunlight. As someone once said, 'Never forget the first rule of holes - when you are in one, stop digging!'

And if things get bad, if you think nobody cares if you're alive, try missing a couple of credit card or loan payments. Only when the last tree has died and the last river has been poisoned and the last fish been caught will we realise we cannot eat money. Waste your money and you're only out of money, but waste your time and you've lost a part of your life.

All of the suggestions in my book can be used for manifesting ANY GOAL OR DESIRE. It just so happens that at this particular time in your life, my Friend, you are focusing on wealth creation because I sense there is a lot of inner turmoil within you taking place right now. People are rightly concerned about their jobs, what will happen with the economy, etc. But do you know what? Sometimes you have to make a conscious choice to tune out of gloom and doom. Even in the best economic times, there is enough of that talk. Make up your mind today to improve your situation in life and it will happen!

The technique that I am about to suggest is a fabulous way to tap into some of your positive and negative beliefs about money. All you do is close your eyes, just imagine a very large blackboard, or whiteboard, in front of you.

Then, on the left side of the board, see all of your positive affirmations concerning wealth. But if at any time you feel the slightest twinge of doubt or disbelief creeping in, like I feel you have had, don't push those thoughts away. Instead, acknowledge them by seeing them appear on the right side of the board. Then, see if you can take those negative thoughts and turn them in a positive direction.

Let me show you how this works with some affirmations and negative beliefs I found in my own head. Here goes:

ON THE LEFT SIDE OF THE BOARD I SEE:
I deserve wealth and I attract it now.

AND ON THE RIGHT I SEE:

Spiritual people shouldn't want wealth. But I want wealth, so does that mean I'm not a spiritual person? Oh, I'm so confused! But I really like this affirmation, so I'm going to keep saying it until it feels right.

ON THE LEFT SIDE OF THE BOARD I SEE:

I deserve wealth and I attract it now.

AND ON THE RIGHT:

OK, it's starting to feel a little better. I know in my head that spiritual people deserve wealth. And my not having to worry about money all the time would free me up to do more positive things with my life.

ON THE LEFT SIDE OF THE BOARD I SEE:

Happiness and sales of my book are soaring! (Applies to me, Steve Richards.)

AND ON THE RIGHT:

I don't know. For some reason, I don't like the word 'soaring'. In my mind, I always associate it with things 'soaring out of control'. Hey...maybe that's the problem, right there. I'm afraid that if my book really became a huge best-seller then I might lose control, somehow. Like I would go soaring off the planet or something. Let me rewrite this and try again.

ON THE LEFT SIDE OF THE BOARD I SEE:

It's safe for me to be a best-selling author. I am a best-selling author.

AND ON THE RIGHT:

Yes, I like this affirmation. Let me try some more.

ON THE LEFT SIDE OF THE BOARD I SEE:
I, Steve, deserve nice things.

AND ON THE RIGHT:
But what did my mam always say? 'The best things in life are free!' Yes, those were her words exactly. Does that mean I can't have nice things if they cost money?

No, that doesn't seem right. Down deep, I know my mam wasn't trying to hold me back from having nice things that cost money.

ON THE LEFT SIDE OF THE BOARD I SEE:
I, Steve, deserve nice things. I am open to all channels of wealth now, including through sales of my book. I desire, I deserve and I attract wealth here and now!

AND ON THE RIGHT:
Yes, those are the affirmations that I know will work for me. But maybe I should add something about it being safe to be wealthy. Safety seems like an important issue for me.

ON THE LEFT SIDE OF THE BOARD I SEE:
I, Steve, deserve nice things. I am open to all channels of wealth now, including through sales of my books. It's safe to be a successful writer, and I am. I desire, I deserve, and attract wealth here and now!

AND ON THE RIGHT:
Yes, I like it. Those are just the affirmations that I know will work for me. And the more I say them, the more they will become my new reality.

The Cosmic Ordering Service

As you can see from the aforementioned, my Friend, a lot of things can come bubbling up to the surface that prevent us from reaching our goals. So this can be a fun and powerful process to try every morning.

Now invent some of your own, my Friend. After a few days of doing this exercise you will then get a good sense of what your real resistance is to creating wealth in your life. And you will also get a sense of what you need to do to break through that resistance to manifest your new reality. But if this process makes you feel uncomfortable for some reason, respect that! It's OK sometimes to just go ahead and make changes in your life - without having to fully understand how you got to be so unhappy in the first place.

Money is neither my god nor my devil. It is a form of energy that tends to make us more of who we already are, whether it's greedy or loving.

Take a minute now, or later, to close your eyes and remember how good it feels to be happy. Recall all the times that fabulous things came your way. Maybe it was a present that you received for your birthday. Or an unexpected bonus at work. Or a bit of good news that arrived in the post. Or an evening that was especially romantic. Just let all those fond remembrances come flooding back to you. Don't worry about the details too much. But instead, capture the essence of happiness. In your mind's eye see yourself smiling, laughing, and celebrating your good fortune. Now, after a few moments of this, open your eyes and affirm to yourself as follows:

I have a hunch that good things are coming my way! Something truly wonderful is about to happen in the next 24-hours!

Affirm that statement often and expect marvellous things to happen. In fact, I wouldn't be at all surprised if something truly dramatic happens to improve your circumstances for the better. But don't question the wisdom of the Universe. Don't look the proverbial gift horse in the mouth. It may be that you get a little sign at first that your fortunes are about to change. Perhaps you find money in the street. Or you get an unexpected compliment from your employer. Or you hear from a friend who has some good news to share with you. And maybe in this way you realise that if things can improve for your friend, they most certainly can improve for you.

Also, stay open to any other hunches that come through. Your ESP powers (sixth sense) will direct you to your good if you let them!

You've probably heard me say this before in my newsletters, so forgive me if I am repeating myself. Some people have some strange ideas about ESP. One of the mighty myths about extrasensory perception is that it somehow works like an electrical switch. Turn the switch and you are instantly all-knowing. Then after spouting some fabulous prediction, you turn the switch off and go blank like a television set.

Well, the real world doesn't work that way. At least that's not how it works for me. In a sense, the switch is always on. Think of it like a television set that is constantly playing in the background as you go about your daily chores. Sometimes you may make a conscious effort to tune into something that is important to you. Sometimes you block out the background noise and forget the TV is even on. But whether you care to listen or not, channels of information are always available to you.

At times it may seem strange and confusing because you catch only a tiny snippet of a 'news report'. In this way, you know something bad has happened to a loved one without knowing all the precise details. In a similar fashion, you may chance upon the tail end of 'tomorrow's forecast' and get a general sense that especially favourable conditions are in the works, and that something really good is about to happen.

Of course! There are times when it will seem like the TV is turned on full blast and you will get amazingly detailed information. Perhaps you'll be warned of an earthquake. Get a message from the other side. Or, sadly, know that someone has passed away before you even get the phone call. Dramatic things like this happen to me frequently.

Yet more often than not, I get an urge to do or not do something without really knowing why. Following my 'hunches' has been a rewarding experience for me. It has enriched my life, personally and professionally. And I am convinced it will do the same for you.

Just don't get hung up on the idea that every hunch has to lead to an immediate windfall. Wealth can come in many forms and some of your hunches may seem to have nothing to do with money until you act on them. For example, you may suddenly find yourself thinking of an old friend, a former co-worker you haven't heard from in years. The urge to call this person keeps getting stronger and stronger. The problem is you don't have their number! But then you get another hunch to go to a certain restaurant. There you run into a mutual friend who just happens to know where your former co-worker is living (synchronicity).

So finally, you call up your old friend and in passing you learn of a fabulous position that is just opening up. Not only are you the ideal candidate, but also this new job has a very high salary! And all this comes about because a former co-worker just 'popped' into your head. Trust me - things like this can and do happen when you listen to that *inner voice*!

Imagine for a moment how you would really feel if all of your desires centred on wealth became reality, my Friend? Would you be as happy as a kid at Christmas time? Would you dust off some of your old dreams and take another chance at honestly living your heart's desires? How would you be around other people? My guess is you would be amazingly patient with people, extra loving, and extra kind. Most of us have a natural generosity of spirit and, when we don't have to worry so much about paying the bills, this giving part of ourselves automatically shines through. So what is it that you have right now to give to the world? Are you genuinely appreciating all that the world is giving you now?

My mam was right about one thing: some of the best things in life are free. Beautiful sunsets exist for the poor man/woman as well as the rich. Take time today to enjoy one! And as you watch the sunset, think of all the good that you have accomplished in your life. Think too of all the blessings you have. Sometimes we get so busy with the hustle and bustle of life that we forget to stop and enjoy things like sunsets and sunrises. And the lovely stars at night. We forget to thank our higher power for the beauty of it all.

At a subatomic level, we and everything else in the Universe is Energy. When you break everything down, we're all made of the same stuff, and we're all connected. The Universe is just this huge ocean of Energy, vibrating at various frequencies which give the illusion of individuation. That is, we experience the illusion of separateness from each other, physical objects, and wealth because our 'senses' are decoding the Energy around us in such a way as to create our physical reality.

So, to simplify things quickly here for the sake of time (another illusion), 'things' only exist because we observe them. It is in our observing that things come into existence. Without our observing, things are simply 'waves' - probabilities of existence. Physicists agree on this.

Our beliefs are a very powerful Energy system in our lives. Our beliefs allow or disallow certain experiences in our lives, including wealth. They make up whom we are. We 'BE' in the world according to our beliefs. If we are being is 'someone who is trying to get wealthy by repeating affirmations' then THAT is what our reality will be. We will just be TRYING to get wealthy.

We have to make the decision that we ARE wealthy, contrary to any external physical evidence. That evidence is an illusion based on the belief systems that have guided who we have been 'being' up to that point.

A truly wealthy person isn't wealthy because they have money. They have money, because they are wealthy! Here's an example I found to illustrate what I mean:

Tommy Bloggs became a millionaire at a very young age. Then, due to a series of poor judgments, he lost it. But within a year, he had it back. How did he do this? HE NEVER LOST HIS WEALTH. He only lost his money, which is just a symbol of wealth! Because he is 'Wealth Conscious', he literally 'magnetically attracts' wealth into his life. He truly can't help it! It's who he is! And there are thousands out there like him, who attract wealth simply because it's who they are. You can make the same decision and have the same results.

Conversely, a person who has grown up with a 'lack of consciousness' can win millions in the lottery and lose it within a year. Their consciousness - their ENERGY - simply can't maintain the attraction to Wealth because they aren't 'wealthy' in who they are being.

Wealth is simply a decision away. If you aren't currently experiencing wealth, you first need to realise

50

that abundance is everywhere...in fact, it's all there is. Poverty and lack are the illusions. You can shift your consciousness to Wealth - BE Wealth - by simply making the decision, THEN your thoughts, speech, and action will allow you to experience the wealth that is yours!

This is, indeed, a complex subject which challenges our core belief systems. But it is those very belief systems that keep a person in a state of lack. Look at your financial situation today. Look at your core beliefs about Wealth and You, and see if your life isn't a PERFECT reflection of your beliefs. Then, look where those beliefs may have originated. When you can awaken to yourself that your beliefs create your reality, rather than the other way around, you have the option to truly be free to experience a reality of prosperity that you deserve!

That is the key to how you can unlock the door to riches. Forget the self-recrimination and chastisement. Start with a new outlook, cleanse your chakras and start anew.

My Friend, remember this in your Orders:

"Cosmos is my unfailing supply, and large sums of money come to me quickly, under grace, in perfect ways.

"As I grow in a financial consciousness, I should demand that the enormous sums of money, which are mine by divine right, reach me under grace and as appropriate, in perfect ways.

"I have within myself a gold nugget; it is my consciousness of gold, of opulence, which brings riches into my life."

Let me use a popular example. A man was spending the night in a farmhouse. The windows of the room had been nailed down, and in the middle of the night he felt suffocated and made his way in the dark to the window. He could not open it, so he smashed the pane with his fist,

51

drew in draughts of fine fresh air, and had a wonderful night's sleep.

The next morning, he found he had smashed the glass of a bookcase and the window had remained closed during the whole night. He had supplied himself with oxygen, simply by his thought of oxygen.

When a student of Cosmic Ordering is able to let go of his/her problem (cast his/her burden) he/she will have instantaneous manifestation. One should always follow a denial with an affirmation.

I am asked so often the difference between visualising and visioning. Visualising is a mental process governed by the reasoning or conscious mind; visioning is a spiritual process, governed by intuition, or the super conscious mind. The student should train his/her mind to receive these flashes of inspiration, and work out the 'divine pictures', through definite leads. When a man/woman can say, 'I desire only that which Cosmos desires for me,' the Master Architect within gives him/her his/her new set of blueprints.

Becoming rich might seem like an overwhelming problem, but it can be done. You can't expect it to be fixed overnight, but you can fix it with a careful plan. By looking at the big picture, you will see where you can save even the smallest amounts of money and all those small amounts will eventually add up to a huge chunk of money over time. I know this is not going to be met with satisfaction on your part, but you are asking for something to fall out of mid-air and land at your feet without any planning as to how it will happen.

Formulate a plan with a clear path to your goal, all laid out, stick to it by getting into new saving and spending habits and then it's just a matter of time till you get your freedom back. Once you get back your freedom, learn from your lesson by sticking to your new way of life and then sit back and enjoy.

Is it a problem that drags you down daily? If so, you are not alone; in England, in this one year, there are millions of working people who have accumulated credit card debt in excess of their present ability to pay.

No matter what task you've chosen to accomplish, you will feel yourself becoming a more powerful, confident, and dynamic person as this programming process continues.

Here's the open secret to manifestation: your success depends on where you place your attention. In everyday life, our attention is scattered. It's on our bills, on whether we can get the kids to school on time, on whether we're going to get a promotion, and dozens of other things, all at the same time. This is the Beta mind state: the everyday mind state, perfect for multi-tasking, but not for making the connection.

You see, this is why I was so angry when people were going on TV and saying you just had write your desires down on a bit of paper and forget all about it! Yikes, what rubbish! Some degree of effort is required in the sense that you have to work on ridding yourself of negativity, some people can do this within minutes and some never quite manage to do it.

When our ability to distinguish the reality of an experience is suspended, we more readily fantasise, have more constructive visualisations and begin to believe that the synthetic images are actually real.

Meditation can be an open door to psychic experiences of many kinds and usually involves turning our attention inward to the mind itself, which emphasises mental activity invoking the guidance of a higher power.

Differentiating between prayer, which emphasises communication with a higher being, and meditation, which focuses on developing oneself, it is important to understand that such meditation can induce an altered state that will help you gain what you want.

The Cosmic Ordering Service

I know this is not, perhaps the answer you wished for. I do wish I could make it happen as you want it.

You need to learn how to relax more. So there you have it, my Friend, probably about £1,000 worth of free advice, I hope you take it and can then move on to placing Orders within the bounds of your own scope.

Nailing down specifics in your Order is far better, but use clean language. Go for it!

A Word About Relationship Abuse

Abuse comes in many forms. Most people think of abuse as being under physical attack: hitting, punching, kicking, pulling hair, twisting limbs, pinching, slapping, biting, etc.

There are many other types of abusive behaviour which hurt just as much as, if not more than, physical abuse.

There are many types of abuse which are just as destructive as physical abuse.

Children can endure years of abuse, too. Without entering into emotive content it is easy for you to imagine what pain children go through in later years because of what they have endured…silently.

Witnessing abuse as a child is something that stays with you all of your life…I should know, having witnessed some of the worst sort of abuse a child could be party to - seeing his mother beaten violently by her husband.

Attacks do not just have to of a physical nature, they can be emotional, verbal and psychological. Such abuse can start a chain reaction of events that can end up involving all sorts of professional agencies, as well as family and friends.

Many of those abused choose to do nothing and suffer in silence. Sometimes the alterative is just as bleak as staying with the abuser. Fear of what could happen to their children is often a key component as to why the victim continues to cohabit with the perpetrator of abuse.

Sometimes the answer is not as easy as you would think. Developing interests and close relationships outside the realm of an abusive spouse/lover in order to escape from an abusive relationship sometimes isn't possible, as the abuser may feel threatened and can become worse.

55

Conquer Destructive Abuse

Destructive abuse is violence to pets or property: throwing things, punching holes in walls, stomping on things which he/she has thrown to the floor, pounding fists on doors or tables to generate fear, breaking doors or windows to get to partner, destroying partner's personal property or keepsakes, injuring or killing pets.

I have personally experienced being a victim of such abuse as a child when my pet rabbit, Snowy, was killed by a boyfriend of my mother. I can tell you, it is soul destroying!

The abuser may be 'addicted to drama' since it creates excitement. This behaviour is damaging because it puts you always on edge. You're always waiting for the other shoe to drop, and you can never know what's expected of you. You must remain hyper-vigilant, waiting for the other person's next outburst or change of mood.

"Heal the past, let personal truths be painless. Let me develop my own viewpoints and validate my own feelings and perceptions. Allow my feelings of what is going on around me become even more familiar and conformable, and that way I can regain control from the destructive abuser.

"I can become even more powerful in coping with my feelings, let this shine through to others. I am a worthy person, let others see this in me. Let others value me with positive treatment, as appropriate.

"I will be able to illicit good behaviour from those around me by my joy that permeates through to them. My powerful words will be responded to with respect and acceptance."

Conquer Economic Abuse

This form of abuse is far more common than you would think. Withholding money as a punishment and making a partner beg for necessities, demanding a partner to relinquish rights to her/his own income and requiring a partner to account for all money spent (down to the exact penny) are all forms of economic abuse.

Economic Abuse means having no access to the family's money. It implies that the abusive partner maintains control of the family finances, deciding without regard for the other person how the money is to be spent or saved, thereby reducing the woman/man to complete dependence for money to meet her/his personal needs.

Even though a woman/man may live in a comfortable home, wear good clothing or have children who are well-equipped with toys and luxuries, she/he may have no control over what monies come into the family, or over any decisions about what will be bought.

"I know I can make my very own strategic plan on maximising my financial resources and making sure that every penny earned is well spent. I want to move on to being able to take charge of coordinating my finances and listing all expenditures that may affect the way I use my income. Empower me to take charge of my economic stability as an individual.

"Already I can have control over my source of income, lifestyle, spending habits, current job and house location, cost of living, payables and loans. Let me determine my level of budgeting needs. Starting today, I want to take charge of my finances. I am becoming more successful in a field of self-fulfilment and success."

Conquer Emotional Abuse

Name-calling, mind games, 'crazy-making', belittling, shaming, extreme manipulation, coercion, rejecting, degrading, terrorising, isolating, corrupting and exploiting are all encapsulated under the heading of emotional abuse.

Emotional abuse accompanies other forms of abuse, but also may occur on its own. Repeated verbal abuse such as blaming, ridiculing, insulting, swearing, yelling and humiliation has long-term negative effects on a person's self-esteem and contributes to feelings of uselessness, worthlessness and self-blame.

Emotional abuse can have serious physical and psychological consequences for men and women, including severe depression, anxiety, persistent headaches, back and limb problems, and stomach problems. Women who are psychologically abused but not physically abused are five times more likely to misuse alcohol than women who have not experienced abuse.

"I want my self-esteem to be boosted even more. Whilst others around me are full of themselves, I can resist with a strong spirit that is within me. I want to become a person worthy of praise, and for others to see that I am blameless, caring, loving, humble and able to stand up for myself.

"I seek a new way of being perceived by others, and that my strength of character be my best defence when needed in these situations, as appropriate. Let the joy of life that is within me come to the surface, and whenever I need joy to be there then let it be in abundance.

"If needed, give me the strength to walk away to a new life that is far better. Let it show that I mean what I say, give me the strength to say what I mean."

Conquer Humiliation Abuse

This type of abuse borders on intimidation - inappropriate humour designed to put down a partner; public criticism of appearance, parenting skills, housekeeping or cooking skills; pushing someone's face into a bowl of food (or worse); forcing food or other objects into someone's mouth; public showing of embarrassing photos or video clips.

Humiliation of one person by another is often used as a way of asserting power over others, and is a common form of oppression or abuse. Sexual humiliation also falls into this category.

Psychological violence leaves no scars and no physical evidence. Most commonly the violence takes the form of verbal abuse and emotional abuse including trivial nit-picking criticism, constant fault finding combined with a simultaneous refusal to recognise, value, acknowledge and praise.

"Give me the strength to challenge the humiliation from my partner. I want to approach this directly, head on, and ensure my words are heard. I will automatically, as appropriate, come up with a successful plan to find a solution to regain control over my life.

"Show me how to put into practice the powerful methods that obtain the results I want to have happen. Let me reach the decisions I need to reach with ease.

"As an individual I deserve respect and the right to my own private space, this is what I want. Make my words heard by my partner by giving me the power to express myself. Make me strong enough to control situations with my partner. Let me have the choice to stay or go."

Conquer Intimidation Abuse

Suggesting that a partner is inferior or 'less than'; cruel remarks about partner's looks; ridiculing partner's ideas; using gestures, angry looks, loud voice, or cursing to control or cause fear, yelling and screaming. All these things come under the heading of intimidation abuse.

Controlling through scare tactics and oppression shows a power imbalance within the relationship. This really is a type of bullying that causes many victims to leave their homes. In some situations, there may be things you can do to solve the problems yourself. But you should never put yourself in danger.

You need to build a support group around you, make a few lists with phone numbers of people who you can talk to and keep them in your home, bag or car - so that you can call them quickly. Put their numbers into memory on your phone. Remember, if your partner has been diagnosed with a personality disorder then no amount of Cosmic Ordering will help you. However, let's see if this Order will help.

"I want to stop the regime pattern my partner applies to me. My psyche is becoming stronger, I have faith in the changes I will make.

"I want to be steered away from focussing on these occurrences. Direct my energy at maximising my influence to reach my partner. Give me control over my emotions so that I can build a rapport with my partner in letting them know what I want out of the relationship.

"Create a powerful influence within me so that I can get my message across to my partner at every opportunity, as appropriate. Give me the power to gain agreement and commitment from my partner."

Conquer Isolation Abuse

This involves the way others limit your phone calls, or visits to or from friends and/or family. The abuser listens in or even goes as far as 'bugging' phone calls; restricts access to telephone, mail, car, or people; monitors all incoming and outgoing mail; forbids partner to leave the house unless given permission or accompanied by abuser.

The abuser will control whom the victim sees, where she/he goes, whom she/he speaks to and what she/he does. This can take the form of simply not allowing her/him to have her/his friends round or visit her/his family, or ensuring it simply isn't worth it by being in a bad mood because she/he left some housework undone, making her/him feel guilty that she/he was out enjoying herself/himself while he/she worked.

"Let me decide on the friends I want to see. Even though I care dearly for my close family and partner, let my friends know how much I care for them, too.

"Let my partner see how much I care for them, even more than I care for my friends and extended family. Let me take back control over my life, allowing me to feel good about getting out and seeing others I care to see.

"My social support network is coming to my aid, let this happen even more from now on. Show me how to impart to my partner that I understand his/her past ways of showing how much they love me by what they did, and let that now allow me to enthuse them about how they too can change for the better towards me.

"From this point onwards I want to depend more on myself and be able to have authority over communications I have with others in all ways, as appropriate. I AM taking control over that NOW. I am Me again."

Conquer Sexual Abuse

This relates to relationships. The abuser forces their partner to have sex at any time, any place the abuser desires; demands sexual acts that are uncomfortable or distasteful to partner; physical abuse to sexual organs; subjects partner to pornography or bizarre sexual activities; degrades partner's body.

Sexual abuse can be defined as any sexual encounter without consent and includes any unwanted touching, forced sexual activity, be it oral, anal or vaginal/penile, forcing the victim to perform sexual acts, painful or degrading acts during intercourse (e.g. urinating on victim), and exploitation through photography or prostitution.

The abuser may insist on sex following a physical attack for the victim to 'prove' she/he has forgiven him/her. Whatever form of coercion is used, be it physical, financial or emotional, any sexual act which is not based on mutual consent constitutes sexual abuse.

"From now on I only want things to happen when I ask to happen. Strengthen my resolve to make it known to my partner what I want from the relationship I am in. I am taking back control over my sexual life.

"I control my own desires and sexual acts. My sexual behaviour is determined only by ME. I am the sole person in charge of what I desire, I do what I enjoy doing.

"I will initiate sex at my desired time, making it something I enjoy doing, let my strong will take control over this.

"I am in charge over my body and what I do with it, as appropriate. This is communicated to others by my newfound body language, sending out the right signals."

Conquer Stealth Abuse

This form of abuse is the opposite of verbal abuse. It is often in the form of refusing to communicate, using silence as a weapon to manipulate. It is pretence of ignorance and evasive responses.

Most abusers abuse surreptitiously. They are 'stealth abusers'. You have to actually live with one in order to witness the mistreatment.

In these relationships, such abuse creates pain and trauma and can lead to physical illness. Ongoing abuse is stressful, no matter how much one tries to ignore it. Stress compromises the immune system, leaving the abused person vulnerable to a host of illnesses. Back pain and exhaustion are often the first symptoms.

Stealth abuse sometimes goes unnoticed, even by the victims themselves, until it is too late. Ambient abuse penetrates and permeates everything - but is difficult to pinpoint and identify. It is by far the most dangerous kind of abuse there is.

"I welcome the unknown, as appropriate. I only want good omens in my life. I want to increase my self-worth, self-esteem and self-confidence. I want to learn to trust those around me that I instinctively know I can trust. I can bear great psychological pressures and I am becoming impervious to criticism and judgment.

"Increase my faith in my ability to meet life's demands. Let me learn to trust my senses, skills, strengths, friends, family, and the predictability and benevolence of my environment. Let my senses be heightened so that I can detect truth with ease. I can accept reality for what it is. I already depend upon myself, and I can do so even more."

Conquer Threat Abuse

This may sound like a rather bizarre type of abuse, but when you consider what it entails you will be able to better understand why it is listed in this book. You would be surprised how many emails I receive that relates to this.

Threat abuse can involve the abuser threatening to leave or end the relationship, to commit suicide or harm someone else, to take the children, to spread lies about their partner, to hurt or kill their partner or partner's family/friends, to ruin partner financially, to destroy personal property or kill pets, to reveal secrets or confidential conversations.

To some, this may seem an invisible sort of abuse that doesn't really warrant a page in this book. However, it would seem that the consensus amongst some of you is that it really is a problem.

"I am blameless, as appropriate, in what I am enduring from this threat abuse. My beliefs make me happy, I am now better at protecting my feelings, let that trait become stronger within me.

"Give me the opportunity to examine, in the most accepting environment, the protective beliefs I once had. I now want to understand why my partner uses these powerful words. Let this open a new possibility of forgiveness and compassion. With love in my heart I know I have the choice to love and be happy with my partner.

"I want to transform my life, give me the clarity and confidence to do so. Increase my personal influence, persuasive power and charisma. Let me understand my partner's core values, give me robust strategies in place to deal with them."

Find a Soul Mate

The media has romanticised the idea of a soul mate to epic proportions, and the entertainment arts (movies, songs, etc) have romanticised love in a way that people have created false impressions of a true definition of soul mate.

If you're making a choice based upon an intellectual and emotional basis - without regard for the spiritual or your soul – you'll be making a choice without spirit, or without soul.

Take the word 'soul', add the definition with the definition for 'mate', and you've got a strong definition of a soul mate: the core spiritual nature, immortal, inseparable even from death, fated to be together.

"I seek spiritual synchronicity, trust, and loyalty from a soul mate. I already know my soul mate, we will make each other more powerful as a team than when we're apart.

"I will recognise my soul mate when I see him/her, we are both aware of our spiritual nature. We will be focused on our purpose for being together, our family, career, and other things will always follow in some priority after this purpose.

"I want to know my soul mate through the way our spiritual journeys interrelate and coincide with each other. By seeing how they put the team/partnership journey above their individual journey and desires, let this be a sign that they are my soul mate.

"I want there to be mutual trust and respect. With trust and respect comes the ability to realise aspirations - both as a couple and as individuals. Let my soul mate help to awaken my soul, let him/her into my life now."

Find Lesbian Love

There's a lot wrapped up in your first time lesbian sexual experience. Whether it's your first time having sex at all, or your first time having sex with another woman, being nervous is normal.

The stereotype is that lesbians don't date, they just move from one relationship to another. Whereas there is some truth to every stereotype, don't be worried that just because you came out of the closet, you're going to have a new roommate next week!

Some women have luck meeting partners in bars. Personal ads can be a great way to meet other women. You can place an ad in the local paper or on the Internet. Just like heterosexual folks, your best bet in meeting someone is through a shared activity or common interest. Join a lesbian reading group. Volunteer at the local homeless or animal shelter. Join a women's bike riding club. Volunteer at a gay rights organisation or for a gay-supportive politician.

"I want to engage in consensual sexual activities that bring me and my potential partner pleasure. I want to be able to pick up on the signals of other lesbian women and allow flirtation to pass between us. My self-esteem is high, make it even easier for me to accept my sexuality.

"When I meet a potential lover, let humour loosen both of us up so that I can feel good enough to turn her on. I want to spend time one-on-one with her and to instinctively know what excites her. More importantly, I want to be able to tell her what turns me on.

"I want my first time with a lover being about getting to know her body, getting to know how to turn her on and learning what my chemistry is."

Find Male Homosexual Love

The gay rights movement has been instrumental in changing attitudes about homosexuality. The first social movement to advance the civil rights of gay people was founded in Germany in 1897. It wasn't until the 1960s that organised gay rights groups around the world made headway.

If you struggle with homosexuality and feel trapped, there is hope. The journey is long and the landscape may be pitted with obstacles. Despite the potential difficulty, freedom abounds for those willing to go with their feelings.

"I want a happy integration with the gay and heterosexual community, I want to be accepted by all. I want a level of comfortable respect and self-respect in the society around me. I ask that my path of self-wholeness will lead to spiritual well-being.

"I am strong willed and can accept being gay, I have pride in my sexuality, allow that to be something I am unashamed about.

"I want to meet other men of the same sexuality, being gay is part of who I am. When I meet another man, a potential partner, I want it to be about being physically attracted, and include the need to love and be loved - it can be an emotional need as well as a physical need.

"When I have sex with a new partner, I want to have 'safe sex', and when I get to know them better and become a couple then I may consider having sex in a natural way. I want to listen to my deepest feelings and learn more about what being gay means.

"I want to feel comfortable about looking for gay love."

Find Spiritual Awakening

Look at the trials of your life with a spiritual approach: until your heart has been broken to the things of this materialistic world, you can't open your heart into the higher world.

An awakening allows the possibility of growth to new levels of psychological and spiritual maturity. Now, that doesn't mean you should feel compelled to go out and try to get your heart broken or seek after trials and disasters so you can grow from them.

An 'awakening' is a moment of clarity in which a new insight or understanding is gained. With this new awareness the experience of life is seen differently, and new possibilities are opened. Changes in patterns of thought, emotions, and behaviour occur.

Don't worry; the world is very good at creating just the right challenges for you! Suffering teaches you compassion. Suffering inspires you to contemplate and reconsider your thoughts and actions. Suffering brings renunciation, and renunciation is an important quality for spiritual growth.

"I have arrived to a time when things get better. I ask for a better understanding and state of mind, and for divine beneficence to come into my life.

"I want to be open and receptive to whatever comes up in life. Let my earthly existence generate spiritual power within me so I can leap into a greater vision of what is going on beneath, behind, beyond, and above this pilgrimage of mine.

"What my soul has endured will bring greater meaning and depth of spirit to my life. Give me more appreciation and gratitude for all I have."

Overcome Depression

I start this by strongly advising anyone diagnosed with clinical depression not to use this Order. You might be receiving medication that could block your ability to connect with the Cosmos.

For many, the weight of the difficult spiritual path they have undertaken in life becomes too much to bear. This may manifest as dark periods where suicide seems the only solution to ending their pain. So if you are thinking of committing suicide, or if you have already attempted it, you owe it to yourself to find out why.

Almost anybody can develop the illness; it is certainly NOT a sign of weakness. Depression is also treatable. You may need to see a doctor, but there are things you can do for yourself or things you can do to help somebody suffering from the illness. Always consult a doctor if symptoms of depression persist.

"I want my stress hormones to return to the normal count that will restore my positive feelings. I want to ditch depression. Let the system in my brain that is known as the serotonin or 5-HT system return to normal nerve impulse function. Let molecules of happiness be released into my system.

"Let my serotonin levels be controlled through diet that will include omega-3 fatty acids, vitamin C and Complex carbohydrates, as appropriate.

"Allow my memories to be strong and enable me to access true memories. I am feeling better quickly and having relief will continue to happen. I want to beat and stop it by normalising the levels of neurotransmitters in my brain. Let that start from now onwards."

Overcome Fears/Phobias

A specific phobia is an intense fear of something posing little or no actual danger. Common specific phobias are of closed-in places, heights, escalators, tunnels, motorway driving, water, flying, dogs, blood and insects. Such phobias aren't just extreme fear; they are irrational fear of a particular thing.

Most of us have a few minor irrational fears. Some get nervous at the thought of getting on an airplane. Others shriek at the sight of a mouse. But if your fears are so intense that they interfere with your day-to-day living, you may have a phobia. I have a particular fear, if you can actually label it that, of being around people that sneeze! The problem is I know that the vibrational power of a sneeze can cause a lot of problems to my own vibrational level, and it can spread bacteria up to a 30ft radius! Ah well, I suppose I could place an Order like the one below.

"In my seeking desensitisation to (name it) I will be able to control myself in a calm and safe way. I want to come to terms with a gradual encounter of the object, first in my imagination and then in reality.

"I seek an increase in awareness of control over this exposure that I can combine with relaxation techniques.

"Through repeated experiences of voluntarily facing it, I want to see it and experience it as harmless. With each exposure, I want to feel an increasing sense of control. This sense of control over the fear and the situation and myself will become a most important benefit to me.

"I want to become desensitised to it and to react with control. I will look on it as an everyday chore from now onwards."

Overcome Guilt

Guilt is a feeling of responsibility or remorse for some offence, crime, wrong, etc, whether real or imagined. Guilt is that part of the human conscience that brings us up short and convicts us for actions and thoughts. Guilt is an inherent human trait that should be seen as a gift. However, most of us do not see it as such and, rather than deal with guilt, we naturally attempt to squelch it. However, guilt is that nagging voice within us all that is like water upon a stone, and is meant to bring us to a realisation that there is a standard and we have fallen short, but whose standard is it?

Seeing guilt in its proper light allows us to understand that it is a safety valve for the human condition. Guilt means there is a right and wrong way for us to operate and there are standards of what is good and what is worthy of guilt. The guilt 'gene' is something that we are born with.

"My standards are high, I can forgive myself through the mental strength I am asking for. I want to do things that have positive consequences for others and myself. I will overcome guilt.

"Let me let go of the need to always be in control. Sometimes it's good to let go, let me enjoy those feelings. Allow me to feel good about myself and to be able to take responsibility solely for my own actions. I am guiltless in my own legal actions, let others see this and let it be something I can accept from now on.

"From now on I want to allow the truth into my life and to be a forgiven person. Let my own in-built conscience instinctively know right from wrong.

"I want to wipe out the past by telling you of all those things now (what it is you feel guilty about)."

71

Overcome Life's Pressures

Let's face it: some of you are living in life's pressure pot, whether that be at work or at home. This is hypertension at its worst. If only you knew what it was doing to your internal organs! Organ damage in hypertensive patients is related to their increased average blood pressure and greater 24-hour blood pressure variability. Are you interested in halving your chances of having a heart attack or stroke? Then routinely check your blood pressure and work to lower it if it is high, as this is a by-product of fast living.

Though hypertension patients may not feel ill, they are nevertheless headed for trouble if they do not get their blood pressure under control. An ounce of prevention is worth a pound of cure, as the saying goes.

Do not underestimate the benefits to be had from a healthy diet, exercise, and weight maintenance. Even though these 'treatments' are not medication they offer a similar, if not more effective, result, improve your overall physical and mental health, and have no negative side effects (many medicines do!).

"I want to proactively improve my physical health and make necessary lifestyle changes. Allow the blood in my body to flow through my arteries and veins at a normal pressure, let my health system regulate this automatically. Ensure the elasticity of my arterial system become as flexible as it was in my youth.

"I want a systolic pressure of less than 140mmHg and a diastolic pressure of less than 85mmHg. I no longer become perplexed at situations, allowing myself to relax more and take things in my stride. Tomorrow is always another day, things will eventually get done with ease."

Overcome Loneliness

Loneliness is not necessarily being alone. We may be alone for long periods without feeling at all lonely. On the other hand, we may feel lonely in a familiar setting without really understanding why. The best way to begin to understand loneliness is to examine some of the ways people experience it. You may feel lonely when you feel that you're lacking attachments you had in the past, you are facing changes in your life - a new school, town, job, or other changes, you feel there's no one in your life with whom you can share your feelings and experiences, your self-perceptions are that you're unacceptable, unlovable, not worthwhile.

Loneliness can be made more intense by what you tell yourself it means. Remember, loneliness is not a defect; it is a condition of the mind.

"I am less critical of myself. I want to be positive and praise myself often, as I deserve it. I want to regain my control over my sense of desire and motivation and to get involved in new situations that I will instinctively evaluate as being meaningful. I have important needs that I want satisfied. I will become better at identifying which needs I want fulfilled in a specific situation.

"I want to develop a circle of friends, or a special friend. I will instinctively know when I can learn to do things for myself, and learn to feel better or more content about myself in general.

"In doing the things I ordinarily do in the course of my daily schedule, I will find that I can look for ways to get involved with people. I want to put myself in new situations where I will meet people. Engage in activities in which I have a genuine interest in a natural way."

Overcome Panic Attacks

Panic disorder is a serious condition that usually appears during the teens or early adulthood, and while the exact causes are unclear, there does seem to be a connection with major life transitions that are potentially stressful: graduating from university, getting married, having a first child, and so on.

A panic attack is a sudden surge of overwhelming fear that comes without warning and without any obvious reason. It is far more intense than the feeling of being 'stressed out' that most people experience. Symptoms of a panic attack include a racing heart, difficulty breathing, paralysing terror, dizziness, nausea, chest pains, chills, hot flushes, tingling sensations, fear that you are going mad.

You probably recognise this as the classic 'flight or fight' response that human beings experience when we are in a situation of danger. But during a panic attack, these symptoms seem to rise from out of nowhere. They occur in seemingly harmless situations - they can even happen while you are asleep.

"I want my biological functions within my body to be restored to a healthy, normal function. I want to learn that when I exercise or experience other stimulation that the bodily feelings I have are acceptable, as appropriate.

"I want to be able to isolate the different triggers (physical, psychological, and/or physiological) that set off panic attacks. I want to instinctively find situations I feel comfortable with. I know I am sane, allow me to become even more rational in my thoughts, and be normal again.

"I am in charge of my physical Self, I want to be even more so than I am now. I want to break the situation down into small manageable steps, and to master it."

Overcome Test Anxiety

Generally, we all experience some level of nervousness or tension before tests or other important events in our lives. A little nervousness can actually help motivate us; however, too much of it can become a problem - especially if it interferes with our ability to prepare for and perform on tests.

Improving your perspective of the test-taking experience can actually help you enjoy studying and may improve your performance. Don't overplay the importance of the grade - it is not a reflection of your self-worth, nor does it predict your future success. Try the following Order.

"Let me have normal, rational reactions when I sit my exam. Allow my reactions to be rational. I am a total person, worthy of reward. Now is the time to take the exam with my strong, positive thoughts. During the exam I want to relax my muscles, as appropriate. I have the ability to manage time, make that even more so right now. My mind can become unblocked at will, make that so during the exam/test. Make tenseness an ally, a friend; a cue to cope.

"Let me focus on the present; what it is I have to do, and make what I am doing manageable. I know I am getting better and I learning to cope more smoothly as I get closer towards the exam. Make those things I have to remember become easy to unlock when called upon.

"Make my goals the things that motivate me, and what I seek attainable when I ask for an increase in commitment. I want to attain cognitive mastery of the material that will be covered on the test, and that way I can approach the test with confidence."

Overcome Tiredness/Laziness

We all feel tired from time to time. Usually, we know why we are tired. We take the time to rest and we get over it quickly.

For some of us, tiredness can be a more serious problem. It may go on for a long time or can be so bad that we can't do anything at all. Either way, tiredness can stop us from enjoying and getting on with our lives. Tiredness can often be mistaken for laziness.

Tiredness is common - at any given time, 1 in every 5 people feel unusually tired, and 1 in 10 have prolonged fatigue. Women feel tired more than men, and it can be a problem at any age, but is least common in the very young and old. There are many reasons for tiredness: overweight, unfit, stress, underweight, illness, sleep disruption, insomnia, depression, worry, shock, high expectation, over-sleeping, family problems, work, types of drink and food eaten.

"From now on I want to regulate my sleep patterns. I want to take up exercise in a simple way that will regulate my body clock and make my resolve to get things done stronger. I can plan my week with ease. I will find such planning spurs me on to fulfil what I have written out on a week planner.

"Setting realistic goals for myself will aid my recovery. I expect progress to be good, however small it may seem at the time. This is something I want to overcome for my own good, and to have sufficient balance between work and play.

"I want to achieve a more balanced, stress-free lifestyle, have realistic expectations about what I can achieve and aim for a positive life."

Successful Anger Control

Anger is simply a direct feeling response. Anger can also be a secondary emotion. Many people (particularly males) are trained to accept the feeling of anger, but not to accept the feelings that may have preceded it, such as feelings of hurt, fear, or vulnerability. Sometimes when we feel hurt or vulnerable, we immediately jump to anger because that's more acceptable to us. In this context, it becomes a secondary emotion, it's the feeling we can tolerate rather than such feelings as hurt or vulnerability.

Anger is unhealthy when it gets in the way of your functioning or your relationships; if anger is causing you to lose friends, put your job in jeopardy, if people complain to you about your anger, or if you hear people talking about you having a bad temper. These are signs that your anger is getting in your way, and therefore it's unhealthy. So try this Order for size.

"I want to give myself explicit permission to express my feelings, as appropriate. It's right to express them, it's healthy to release these emotions regularly. Doing exercise can allow that release mechanism to work, let the most effective process be when I can combine both the mental and physical effort.

"I want the intention of releasing the anger. Let me intensely attune to what is within me while I do physical activity, as appropriate. Assist me in releasing the anger energy. Rid me of negative energy.

"I ask that I give myself the opportunity to express myself in a safe way. I want to be open to discovering my own dynamic anger-release method. I want to truly forgive those around me who wronged me, starting from this moment onwards. I also forgive myself."

Successful Dating

Dating can be a daunting prospect, do you go out with company or just the pair of you, and where do you take him/her? There are three situations in respect of where you take them: positive, neutral or negative. By that I mean, you can be positive towards yourself and take them into a situation you are comfortable with, but your date is not. For example, bowling with your buddies. A neutral situation would encompass a situation that the pair of you would be comfortable with: a film at the local cinema followed by a meal at a place which is new to both of you. A negative situation is one where your date is familiar and relaxed, but you are not: meeting them at their local hangouts with their friends present.

By taking your new date into a positive situation for you can be a great way to introduce them to your friends, and for letting your date see you relaxed and in a position of control. Of course, this is not so as to belittle your new date, but is a way of showing them the real you. Are you confident enough to do that? Try this Order for love.

"When I take my date out I want to be able to determine if we are right for each other...in a calm and relaxed way. Focusing on the physical attraction between us will help me enough to continue on to a second date, if that is what I want.

"Improve my ability to talk in general terms and about neutral subjects, in a light and fun way. Let the emotional feelings in my mind be thrilling ones, allow those feelings to be perceived to my date.

"Allow my date to get to know all about me, as appropriate. Let me maintain their interest so that they want a second date. Now I am ready, I feel good about it."

Successful Debt Management

Debt hinders your ability to live freely, and can affect everything from personal relationships to physical and emotional health. Debt is a seemingly endless cycle of making, spending and owing money. It drains your bank account and, figuratively, the very life from your body. How did you get into debt, and more importantly, how can you get out of it? It's never too early, or too late, to learn principles of good money management. If the bills in your mailbox and on your desk are dominating your life, with determination and sound advice, it is possible to break free of debt. This is one of the most commonly asked questions I receive from my Cosmic Friends.

"By starting to save, I can achieve my dreams, both now and down the road. I want to prepare for retirement, I want to boost my saving power in the years ahead, and I know this will lead to some adjustments in the future. I want to regain control over healthy finances and to focus on paying off my debts.

"I want there to be hope in putting my finances on a firm foundation. I am clever enough to draw up a budget, including a schedule for repaying of what I owe. I want to be realistic and work out what I can repay and still stay within my budget.

"I want to put a lid on my spending, more in and less out. I will also save on utility services by selecting the best supplier prices I can secure. There is far more choice on fee-free banking and lower overdraft rates, so it makes sense to switch and take advantage of such offers, make me instinctively find the best deal on these. With regard to remortgaging options, if it looks like I can save money then allow me to make the switch."

Successful Ego-boost

A healthy ego is the sum of self-confidence and self-respect. Your ego performs a critical function. It defines your sense of Self. It identifies you as distinct and unique. Personal conflicts and protecting yourself are expressions of ego that inhibit personal effectiveness and make problems difficult to solve.

Weak egos compensate through excessive control and manipulation and the endless search for more power and authority. A person with a weak ego has difficulty learning from others and thus limits the expansion of his/her knowledge base.

With a healthy ego you are more able to relate to others in a compassionate and concerned way, and you feel able to let others take the lead when appropriate.

"I want to be able to deal with reality as it is, and to persist until the goal is achieved and still maintain the necessary flexibility to change. Let me use an open-minded approach, be innovative and willing to learn new methods.

"In my every day chores and work, I now want to use self-confidence as a key part of being a successful person. On observed reality, setting goals and achieving them is something I will find easy to do. I want to use suggestion, visualisation, and effective goal-setting to improve my self-confidence and self-image.

"Let me follow my instincts, let me do whatever I spontaneously feel like doing, as appropriate. Let me keep a grip on my unchanging life-positive practices like keeping fit, meditating (etc). Free my intellect from certain inhibitions and widen my ego to include all. Let that happen from now onwards."

Successful Home Improvements

With the cost of property soaring, many are turning to home improvements as an alternative to buying a new home. As it happens, one of my hobbies is developing properties. I often find the solution to creating extra income from the property is to add an extra bedroom. When enlarging your home, converting the loft is usually simpler than building an extension.

The most valuable asset a home can have is central heating, as it not only boosts the heat but also boosts the value, and this is closely followed by restoration, then a garage, loft conversion, closely followed by an extension. Surprise, surprise! So how can we lessen the likelihood of things going wrong? Try this Order.

"Make the process of matching the right professional to the project more efficient and worry-free. I want quality design and installation in the (name the project, such as new bathroom, etc). Ensure that I/the builders have the expertise to make my plans a reality. Whatever my taste in decoration, I want my dream improvement to come true.

"Make it easy to get those essential jobs done professionally and with the minimum of fuss. I want the work to be affordable and tailored to my budget. Get things moving by improving or adapting my home so I can continue to enjoy living there safely and independently. Assist planning applications to go smoothly by virtue of the anticipation I instinctively have.

"I want to find out if I can obtain a grant for the project, let me instinctively find the right person to ask about this. I want my budget to be enough to do the job, replacing this money with more money that I can easily earn."

Successful In Vitro (IVF)

Are you considering or undergoing In Vitro fertilisation? This infertility treatment involves stimulating the ovaries to release eggs, then retrieving those eggs and fertilising them in a petri dish.

In its simplest term, IVF is simply the uniting of egg and sperm In Vitro (in the lab). Subsequently, the embryos are transferred into the uterus through the cervix and pregnancy is allowed to begin. IVF was the first of the ART techniques to be developed. The first birth was in 1978 in England. The procedure was pioneered by a Gynaecologist and a Ph.D. (Drs Steptoe and Edwards).

Embryos from an IVF cycle can be frozen for your own future use. Along with a big emotional and physical commitment, let this Order be of help to you. Remember, IVF is a procedure that simply mimics what goes on inside the womb. Something that is natural.

One cycle of IVF takes four to six weeks to complete. You and your partner can expect to spend about half a day at your clinic for the egg retrieval and fertilisation procedures. You'll go back two to three days later for the embryos to be transferred to the uterus. The female should place the following Order.

"Allow the manmade drugs I have been given to stimulate my ovaries to develop several mature eggs for fertilisation. My blood hormone levels will be at their optimum, with ease, and they will let my doctor detect when my eggs are mature.

"When my partner's sperm is combined with my eggs, let them be cultured successfully in an incubator. When those embryos are transferred into my uterus through my cervix, let this result in a successful pregnancy."

Successful Internet Dating

There are so many Internet dating sites that you will be spoilt for choice. There are dating sites dedicated to millionaires, disabled, elderly, pet owners, religion and sexuality.

Most dating sites have security and privacy policies and those that don't are best avoided. Ensure that you feel comfortable with security measures in place so that your personal details are never given out, not unless you wish to give these out yourself.

Some cyber daters are looking for a quick flirt or an unusual love adventure, while others are looking for the partner of their dreams, with whom they would like to spend the rest of their lives. Due to the big differences in the aims of people, when two people finally meet they can be disappointed and discouraged. So with the help of this Order let's hope you find love on the Internet.

"Allow my communication with a potential partner via the Internet be powerful. Let my positive energy help my emails get through to them. Let the energy I have put in to them still be within the messages when they open them.

"My high hopes of online romance are to be reflected in my profile that I posted on the dating site. Let it attract potential partners. Let the attracting electromagnetic energy be felt by them when they view my profile. I want to make Internet dating a good way of meeting new people and making friends.

"When I communicate my feelings to potential dates let them know how motivated I am to meet them for real. The sincerity I have within me is a powerful tool, that when used on the Internet attracts potential partners. Let that happen whenever I use Internet dating."

Successful Speed Dating

Speed Dating for three minutes or so might not seem like much, but you'd be surprised how easy it is to see if there's any chemistry with each of the people you meet. You have to find out what tickles the other person's fancy. I hope this helps singles quickly click with someone who will resonate to their intelligence and sense of humour.

Speed dating is a simple way for you to meet other busy professional singles. If you're fed up with not meeting that right person in clubs and bars, blind dates that don't work and the office romance is frowned upon, then this could be the answer. Speed Dating is ideal for those who lead busy lives, don't have much time and want to meet new people in a fun, safe environment.

"When speed dating, let me relax and tune into my instincts. I will find that I am more able to concentrate on how I am feeling within myself.

"When I sit with my date I will be able to say something positive about them: their eyes, smile, voice, clothes, hair - and be able to focus on it and think pleasant thoughts. I will be able to relay these pleasant thoughts to my date without the use of words.

"I am able to mirror my date in gesticulations with ease, and develop the ability to build a rapport with them through unspoken communication.

"I want to be able to use positive and convincing dialogue. I see myself smiling and relaxed during the speed dating session. I see myself giving my date undivided attention, let this happen with ease.

"When each date has ended, and when going on to the next speed date, I will feel just as good and refreshed as when I first started."

Successful Sport Performance

Sports performance enhancement will help you achieve the results you want in the fastest possible time.

Do you find yourself anxious prior to a game, match, or competition? Each of us starts out the day with a certain amount of energy, but if you waste your energy worrying about the competition, about your opponents, etc, by the time you are ready to compete, you feel less than your best.

Do you lose motivation or enthusiasm over time or during a competition? In a team sport, do you find yourself losing your own motivation it the team is playing badly? Do you find your own athletic performance erratic, sometimes good and sometimes bad? Do you worry at times that you are not good enough and lose your confidence? In each of these cases the problem is in your own mind, specifically your unconscious. This Order can help you reverse these negative thoughts.

"When I see myself in my mind's eye performing in (name that sport) I will be perfect, let the same happen when I play for real. I am improving my game of (whatever it is) and I want to set targets for myself that I can achieve.

"I want to become the best at (name it) and to claim my rightful success. I will learn how to focus myself on my game. I want my reaction times to improve, and to improve my training by creating a personal 'trigger' that can help me train more consistently with proper form and to compete successfully. My muscle action and tone can improve even more than it is, let my muscle-tendon strength increase, and let the techniques of power become second nature to me. Strengthen my body to cope."

85

Successful Weight Loss

If you fully intend to shape yourself up from a couch potato to a fit and healthy individual, some type of exercise activity should be added to your daily routine. While you might be a beginner at a healthy lifestyle it does not necessarily mean you should not get the most out of your workout.

One of the things to consider is when and what to eat so that you can get the maximum out of your workout plan. Always consult a doctor before commencing a workout regime if you have been inactive for a number of years.

"I enjoy healthy exercise, and I enjoy good health. I will naturally become fitter than I already am. Allow that to continue, as appropriate. I eat regular small, healthy meals throughout the day, or a cereal bar or a sports drink or a fruit juice rich with carbohydrates, allow it to improve my performance doing things that contribute to weight loss. I enjoy the correct portions of healthy oil that are in nuts or oil-giving fish, allow those nutrients to sate my appetite.

"Fresh water replenishes and cleanses, allow it to hydrate me where it works best. Allow my system to be able to enjoy healthy intakes of water so that I can feel positive results.

"I look and feel absolutely wonderful, there is a brand new me, as appropriate, that is attractive and positively vibrant. Let my new energy enable me to become more active and fitter. As each day goes by I allow the Cosmos to continue making me attractive to others and myself.

"I ask that my new daily eating allowance be ideal for what I want, and that I will happy with the result that I know will benefit me in weight loss."

A Word about Quitting Drugs

When an occasional habit gets out of control it can soon become an addiction. It doesn't just wreck the life of the abuser; it wrecks the lives of those around them.

An addiction can be controlled, and the sooner it is acted upon then the sooner the abuser can regain their life back.

I have divided this section up to cover a cross-section of drugs, intermingled with some other Orders, as some are classed as 'social/recreational' drugs, some are injected, some are smoked and some are 'necked' (swallowed).

Remember, not all drugs are illegal, as there are just as many that have come to be dependent on prescription drugs, like tranquillisers, painkillers and sleeping tablets.

You will know that you have a dependency on drugs because of what they are doing to your mind and body. Even steroid abuse amongst bodybuilders can be considered addictive, the user never becoming big enough or strong enough as they see themselves in their mind's eye, or the gym mirror.

The pleasant experience that drug users get from taking certain types of drugs can lead to them taking more and more. This book cannot address that sort of addiction, nor could Cosmic Ordering be of any initial use, as the abuser is not likely to be predisposed to want to give them up.

Once physical and mental dependence sets in then professional help has to be sought, but it takes two to tango. The abuser has to be willing. If the abuser does not want to stop taking drugs then they are hooked! There is nothing you can do, short of locking them up. Even those locked up behind bars can still get their supply of drugs!

Quit Antidepressants

Antidepressants are drugs that relieve the symptoms of depression. There are almost thirty different kinds of antidepressants available today and there are four main types:

- Tricyclics
- MAOIs (Monoamine oxidase inhibitors)
- SSRIs (Selective Serotonin Reuptake Inhibitors)
- SNRIs (Serotonin and Noradrenaline Reuptake Inhibitors)

Seroxat is part of a family of antidepressants called SSRIs (selective serotonin re-uptake inhibitor), which were introduced to the market in the early 1990s.

They were a replacement for benzodiazepines such as Valium and Librium - and their selling point was that people would not become physically dependent on them, unlike the older drugs. In spite of not having the symptoms of addiction, up to a third of people who stop SSRIs and SNRIs have withdrawal symptoms.

"Increase my already strong will to live, rehydrate me to the levels needed, as appropriate. Fill me with joy, make me get better quicker without drugs. I want to socialise, carry on working, and enjoy normal leisure activities.

"Allow my partner, family and friends to see me adjust to positive change with ease.

"Let things resolve themselves naturally within days, when I will feel a lot better and stronger with each day. Make happiness and sunny days my therapy."

Quit Boozing

Alcohol weakens the immune system, and creates unnecessary problems within the body by depleting it of vitamins and minerals. The body then desperately fights to function properly. In the realm of skincare, alcohol causes dehydration, which deprives our complexions of precious moisture that is necessary to keep it soft, smooth and youthful.

Alcohol in excess is known to overtax the liver, which is a much-needed organ that helps to diffuse impurities from reaching and harming other organs and systems of the human body. Alcohol consumption can lead to broken or distended capillaries, especially over the nose and cheeks. Many of the social problems we have are caused by alcohol binge drinking, costing the UK health service in excess of £1b per year!

"The control over desire for alcohol has its origins in genetics. I ask that my genetics be attuned to a higher level so that they discover a healthy alternative to such control and that I accept a new way of life.

"Make my neurotransmitters associated with this become more abundant and able to cope with more ease than they have done.

"Let me feel a pleasant and acceptable feeling of control, knowing that I can adequately cope with the changes that are about to take place within me.

"This new stability, by natural means, of dealing with this through a healthy diet supports the replenishment of these neurotransmitters that can ease and increase internal calm. Allow my brain to replenish the chemicals needed within me and to balance the neuro-chemicals in the brain so that I feel comfortable in abstinence of alcohol."

Quit Cocaine

There are basically two chemical forms of cocaine: the hydrochloride salt and the 'freebase'. The hydrochloride salt, or powdered form of cocaine, dissolves in water and, when abused, can be taken intravenously (by vein) or intranasal (in the nose). The freebase form of cocaine is smokable.

Cocaine is generally sold on the street as a fine, white, crystalline powder, known as 'coke', 'C', 'snow', 'flake', or 'blow' (sometimes used to refer to marijuana). Street dealers generally dilute it with such inert substances as cornstarch, talcum powder, and/or sugar, or with such active drugs as procaine (a chemically-related local anaesthetic) or with such other stimulants as amphetamines.

"Even though I am rational, give me more rational brain power. Make me stronger than cocaine, strengthen me. Continue to maintain my cardiovascular and cerebrovascular systems within me as they should be.

"Make neurological functions within me even more able to be rested when I need them to be, and to restart whenever needed in a logical way. I trust those around me, allow that to continue and for the bond I have with my family and friends to grow in trust. The sounds I hear around me are real sounds, let real sounds continue, as appropriate.

"The rhythm of my heart, when rested, is steady and constant, as appropriate, I ask you to let that continue in a good way. I ask that the thoughts in my head be logical and painless ones. Nauseous feelings leaving me even more. Let me feel good and naturally stimulated within myself again."

Quit Ecstasy

Adding to the already existing dangerous potential of ecstasy is the fact that, increasingly, other drugs altogether are being passed off as ecstasy and that ecstasy pills are sold heavily laced with other dangerous drugs such as PCP.

When most people refer to ecstasy they are usually referring to methylenedioxymethamphetamine, or MDMA. Patented in Germany before World War I, MDMA was not tested on humans until the 1970s. Chemically, it's structurally similar to amphetamine and mescaline, a hallucinogen.

"I ask that you give me the controlled feeling of being euphorically high at the appropriate times solely by virtue of my higher Self.

"Rehydrate my physiological Self and make it even better than it has been at controlling my temperature to 36.8 degrees Celsius (plus or minus 0.7 degrees), as appropriated, and in the bodily places this temperature should be. Let my body temperature vary as it needs to during the day, as appropriate, according to my activity level.

"Thank you for making those around me worth changing my situation for. The more I see these family and friends' loving faces, the more I can resist ecstasy.

"I am high on living a good life in a sensible way, I ask you to continue making wonderful and worthwhile things happen for me.

"The detoxifying substance within me is strong, as appropriate, I only have the desire for legitimate highs, let that continue from now onwards."

Quit Gambling

Gambling is like a drug, as it releases certain hormones in the brain that makes the gambler feel good. Despite what the casinos and bookies tell you, nothing is free. Gambling traps you with the possibilities of turning a few pounds into 50, 100, one million. Unfortunately, the success doesn't last and betting robs you of more than just money. It puts your family at a higher risk of experiencing bankruptcy, divorce, suicide, domestic violence and other tragedies. If gambling is destroying your financial resources, causing problems in your marriage and sabotaging your future, then invoke this Order.

"I want to shake off gambling from my life. I want to regain control and restore the balance to my life. I know what it means to my good health. I can learn to reshape things. My family is important to me, more important than anything else. Make them the renewed focus for my attentions. I now want to get my daily fix from knowing how strong I am in my higher Self.

"I want to put money to good use, to a more harmless pastime that will strengthen my resolve to continue on as I want to. I want you to enable me to become more aware of the better things in life by virtue of empowering me.

"I want you to allow me to cooperate with those around me by assisting me to listen to them. Do this by virtue of my seeing and realising how much they love me.

"I want to cast off and stop gambling, as I want to become stronger and be able to resist it.

"I want to find another way to fix my financial situation and see my personal wealth in my life increase by ways that I am proud of. I want to resist gambling and regain my life, and then I can be a winner! I am a winner."

Quit Hallucinogens

Hallucinogens are drugs that cause hallucinations - profound distortions in a person's perceptions of reality. Under the influence of hallucinogens, people see images, hear sounds, and feel sensations that seem real but do not exist. Some hallucinogens also produce rapid, intense emotional swings.

Hallucinogens cause their effects by disrupting the interaction of nerve cells and the neurotransmitter serotonin. Distributed throughout the brain and spinal cord, the serotonin system is involved in the control of behavioural, perceptual, and regulatory systems, including: mood, hunger, body temperature, sexual behaviour, muscle control, and sensory perception.

LSD (an abbreviation for 'Lysergic Acid Diethylamide') is the drug most commonly identified with the term 'hallucinogen' and the most widely used in this class of drugs.

"I want to feel attached to reality, have my perceptions of sight and sound restored and reattach to the environment, nature and my Self, as appropriate.

"Continue to make my life a good trip and stabilise my emotions and senses so that colours, smells, sounds, and other sensations are perceived as they are.

"Make the sensory signals I received from my body be better interpreted and my expectations continue to be good. Let me experience emotions as they happen. I want to be in control and I can without (put the word of the particular hallucinogen here). I dream of good, I know you will make good continue to happen. Good is happening to me right now."

Quit Heroin

Heroin is a highly addictive drug. Recent studies suggest a shift from injecting heroin to snorting or smoking because of increased purity and the misconception that these forms of use will not lead to addiction.

Although less diluted, heroin is becoming more common. Most street heroin is 'cut' with other drugs or with substances such as sugar, starch, powdered milk, or quinine. Street heroin can also be cut with strychnine or other poisons. Because heroin abusers do not know the actual strength of the drug or its true contents, they are at risk of overdose or death. Heroin also poses special problems because of the transmission of HIV and other diseases that can occur from sharing needles or other injection equipment.

"My mind is strong, let my body learn to cope. Make me better able to win this fight. Repair, as appropriate, the scarred and/or collapsed veins. Fight on with good bacteria that are produced within me. Increase the good bacteria within me. Make my blood vessels and heart valves even stronger than they are. Heal abscesses (boils) and other soft-tissue infections, and liver or kidney disease within me, as appropriate, by natural means.

"Lift the heroin's feelings from me, allow my respiratory strength to continue to become stronger. Rejuvenate me within, renew my cells even more than they are renewing now, as appropriate. Let the blood vessels that lead to my lungs, liver, kidneys and brain remain unclogged. Allow my immunity and for the detoxification that is working within me continue and for me to become stronger. I only want what is good for me."

94

Quit Marijuana

Marijuana is no longer the Nation's most commonly used illicit drug! In fact, it is scarcer than it has ever been in the UK. Drug dealers and users are now growing their own varieties of marijuana.

The major active chemical in marijuana is delta-9-tetrahydrocannabinol (THC), which causes the mind-altering effects of marijuana intoxication.

Smoking marijuana deposits several times more THC into the blood than does eating or drinking the drug.

Marijuana use impairs a person's ability to form memories, recall events, and shift attention from one thing to another. THC also disrupts coordination and balance by binding to receptors in the cerebellum and basal ganglia

Depression, anxiety, and personality disturbances are all associated with marijuana use. People trying to quit report irritability, difficulty sleeping, and anxiety. They also display increased aggression on psychological tests.

"Make me even stronger in my resolve to win and encourage my body to continue without THC (tetrahydrocannabinol). Be my medication in curing me, by natural means, and make continued improvements to my memory, attention span, ability to learn and my already good health.

"My respiratory tract, lungs, neck and head are to have their good health safeguarded with a greater tendency to overcome and eliminate contagion I do not want.

"I have raised, with your help, feelings of euphoria and relaxation within me. Make this new feeling appeal to me more and more each day."

Quit Methamphetamine

Methamphetamine, often referred to as crystal meth (smokable form), is a powerfully addictive stimulant that dramatically affects the central nervous system.

Also commonly known as 'speed', 'meth', and 'chalk'. It is a white, odourless, bitter-tasting crystalline powder that easily dissolves in water or alcohol. The drug was developed early in this century from its parent drug, amphetamine, and was used originally in nasal decongestants and bronchial inhalers.

Methamphetamine's chemical structure is similar to that of amphetamine, but it has more pronounced effects on the central nervous system. Like amphetamine, it causes increased activity, decreased appetite, and a general sense of well-being. After the initial 'rush', there is typically a state of high agitation that in some individuals can lead to violent behaviour.

"I want my resistance to methamphetamine to be strong, make start within minutes of this Order. I have pleasurable effects coming on as I ask you to make my desire to win become even stronger than it already is.

"Make my natural high continue and maintain it, as appropriate, as and when desired. Increase my ability to resist fatigue, increase activity and to control my appetite as appropriate.

"Euphoria is my natural high, continue to allow me to trust those close to me and let things that happen around me be what I see. Control my moods. Give me the appetite to eat healthy foods that are good for me.

"Reset my behaviour patterns so I am more tolerable. Purify and cleanse my system, as appropriate. My friends are my new stimulant, allow that to happen NOW."

Quit Painkillers

Painkillers are also called 'analgesics' or 'analgesia'. There are many different types and strengths of painkillers suitable for different types of pain.

If one or more of the following occur they will usually ease off if you stop taking the tablets: nausea (feeling sick), diarrhoea, rashes, headache, dizziness, nervousness, depression, drowsiness, insomnia (poor sleep), vertigo (dizziness), and tinnitus (noises in the ear).

The very drug that was supposed to help you is now hurting you. The pain of injury or the fear of medical treatment has been compounded by the painful discomfort of withdrawal. Warning: opiate addiction is recognised as a central nervous system disorder, caused by continuous opiate intake. Seek early treatment before the downward spiralling takes away your job, family, self-esteem and, ultimately, your life!

"I want to use the normally occurring opiate-like substances in my brain to overcome pain. These are opioid peptides, called enkephalins and endorphins. They are neurotransmitters (chemical messengers) that travel along specific nerve pathways in my brain that process information related to being free from pain, emotional behaviour, and other bodily processes affected by opiates.

"Make me relaxed enough within so I can win, let me gain control and be free to enjoy my recreation time.

"Let soothing music send out sound frequencies to stimulate each chemical naturally within me. Let Beta frequencies stimulate my brain to produce more endorphins, from the music I play. Let Alpha frequencies stimulate my brain to produce more serotonin, as appropriate. Let music sooth and relieve me."

Quit Sleeping Pills

These drugs are known as 'hypnotics', or 'sleeping tablets.' About one in five people have some difficulty with sleeping. However, there are many things you can do to help yourself. This section aims to show you some of them. For example, simple things like winding down before bedtime, avoiding certain foods and drinks, and a bedtime routine can help. Further ways to promote sleep in more difficult cases include relaxation techniques, regular exercise, and sleep restriction. Sleeping tablets are not the best way to help with sleep problems because you can get addicted to them, and they often stop working if you take them regularly. Some brand names are Dalmane (Flurazepam), Halcion (Triaxolam).

"Making it easy for me to sleep naturally is my Order. I want my natural urges to sleep to return, they will return. I have to learn to let go, relax and take a nap whenever I wish.

"Give me the desire to have some relaxation time, and let my positive health return. Participating in things alone or with others brings me joy, so does the rest that comes with sleep, let me take advantage of that.

"Each day that I awake I want to feel refreshed and recharged with an abundance of energy that allows me to work hard at what I like doing. I want to be rewarded with a good night's sleep.

"Let my body attune to its sleep patterns. Let me make my bedroom a more comfortable place and when I am sleeping during the night let it be a restful and repairing time. Let my natural sleep cycle become more involved in my sleep patterns."

Quit Smoking

Smoking has been documented in many studies to be quite detrimental to the skin. Smoking is a nasty habit that progressively creates a premature breakdown of your overall state of health, internally and externally. Cigarettes contain ingredients such as acetone, ammonia, arsenic, formaldehyde and nicotine, which are chemical compounds that are considered to be quite harmful to the human body - imagine their impact on the skin. Smokers tend to have a greyish tinge to their complexion, due to a poor oxygen supply. Dehydration occurs, which then increases the risk of premature wrinkles. Smoking can also slow the healing and regeneration process of the body, which could be harmful if you ever needed surgery.

"I want to be smokefree, that is the best thing I could do right now. Already I have made my mind up, and with you there with me I know how great it would be to have even better health than I already have.

"I picture myself waking up and feeling totally fresher than I do now. Fresh hair, fresh clothes, nice white teeth, fresh breath, clean hands, clean air around me, smokefree. I can do it too, that is what I ask of you, just like all those others before me who have done the same.

"Allow me to cleanse all of those associated items, allow me to be stronger than I am with my willpower being increased. Detoxing by drinking fresh fruit juices and pure water can be accelerated, so long as you are with me to give me strength.

"I ask that my resolve to win becomes stronger, that my feelings of overcoming this increase, and that I will be totally smokefree within days."

Quit Steroids

The major side effects of anabolic steroid use include liver tumours, jaundice, fluid retention, and high blood pressure; others are severe acne and trembling. Additional side effects include the following:

- For men - shrinking of the testicles, reduced sperm count, infertility, baldness, and development of breasts.
- For women - growth of facial hair, changes in or cessation of the menstrual cycle, enlargement of the clitoris, and deepened voice.

Research shows that aggression and other psychiatric side effects may result from anabolic steroid abuse. Many users report feeling good about themselves while on steroids, but researchers report that steroid abuse can cause wild mood swings including manic-like symptoms leading to violent, even homicidal, episodes. Depression often is seen when the drugs are stopped and may contribute to steroid dependence

"Make me a loving person, I want to be able to tolerate people more and accept their friendship. I accept that the Cosmos is invincible, make my judgement in the good that I want to do to my body by giving up steroids just as powerful. Restore my ability to produce natural hormones, as appropriate, without effort.

"Let me accept my body as it naturally is, my mind is powerful and my body can be the same way. Mind and body as one is a powerful tool, make my mind even more powerful than it already is. Let me accept me for what I am…a natural, gifted person."

Quit Sunbathing

There has been extensive research performed over the past thirty years on the sun, and its impact on the human body. Through these studies, we have found that a certain amount of sunlight is needed to manufacture vitamin D within our bodies, which is a definite necessity.

However, after a certain allotment of time, those powerful rays can be very harmful to our body's largest organ - the skin. In fact, if it weren't for sun exposure, say the experts, our skin would stay relatively smooth into our eighties.

Dehydration, fine lines, wrinkles and even skin cancer is caused by excessive exposure to UV rays, which penetrate our atmosphere everyday. Some people are prepared to ignore the cancer risk of too much sun or sun bed exposure!

"The stimulation I get from the ultraviolet rays from the sun that release chemicals in me produce a natural high, but I now ask that I get an even more natural high within me without the sun, as appropriate.

"The endorphins I am releasing into my bloodstream, responsible for the 'feel-good factor', continue to be released in an uplifting and natural way without the sun shining on me, as I shine culturally within myself, as appropriate, already.

"The feelings put me in a good and happy high. I want these relaxing effects I have without the sun to contribute to my skin continuing to be smoother and nicer to look at.

"I value my skin's healthy and good condition, I ask you to protect me from the sun, as I will also do by obtaining and wearing fashionable accessories, like large brimmed sunhats and protective garments."

Quit Tranquillisers

These drugs work on a neurotransmitter system called the GABA (gamma amino butyric acid) system, which is the major inhibitory system in the brain – in other words, it dampens down brain activity.

Benzodiazepines used for anxiety include, amongst others, diazepam (Valium), chlordiazepoxide (Librium), lorazepam (Ativan) and alprazolam (Xanax). Benzodiazepines used to help with sleep include: temazepam, nitrazepam and flunitrazepam (Rohypnol). You may experience withdrawal symptoms if you come off them too quickly. With your doctor's help you may find it useful to slowly decrease the dosage, or cut the tablet down by quarters, taking three-quarters over a period of time and then down to a half and so on until you have reached the final quarter, and then none. Coming off tranquillisers too fast can be dangerous. Consult a doctor.

"I believe I can live without these drugs, I ask you to see me through it and organise my life so that I can manage things even better than I have done. Improving my sleep patterns is something I want. I gain relief from knowing how I can communicate this to you right now.

"Let a gradual and careful release of your healing power in to me, let it replace tranquillisers. I ask that you can support me through this, and that my family and friends will also support me and understand.

"Already I am feeling good, thanks to your care and concern. I want to feel good, I want to feel strong and in control of myself. I can vary and reduce my dose as appropriate.

"The thought of you making discontinuation of these drugs an easy thing for me to do makes me feel good."

Anti-Ageing

Ponce de Leon (1460 – 1521) went to find Bimini, one of the islands in the Bahamas. 'The Fountain of Youth' was supposed to be in Bimini. Legend has it that anyone who drank from the fountain would never grow old. Imagine how life would be if Ponce de Leon really discovered The Fountain of Youth or if there was some type of miracle cream that would completely eradicate all signs of aging. Wouldn't life be sweet?

"My hormones are working fine, staying in good condition for each of the three hundred and sixty-five days of the year, continuously through my long and healthy existence. I have good skin complexion, and with each day, from now to the future evermore, it stays strong. Sebum production in my skin continues to rejuvenate elasticity, as appropriate. My youthfulness remains with me, I have good genetics, and a healthy lifestyle. I am invigorated with even more energy than I already possess. I am always young looking. By continuing to live and maintaining a healthy lifestyle throughout my years, I increase production of beautiful, nubile skin. I have a vibrant complexion and already look beautiful at any age.

"My skin and tissue, as appropriate, regenerate themselves. Foods that provide my body with vitamins and minerals are things what I want on my plate. I develop and maintain a healthy glow. I enjoy oils that maintain proper function of all tissues and tissue repair, especially the skin, when I eat my correctly portioned meals that have a good nutritional value.

"Allow the fountain of youth to replenish my vigour and pep on a daily basis."

Parenting Attention Deficit
Hyperactivity Disorder ADHD

ADHD has become a label seemingly affixed to every hyperactive or distracted child. Though young boys and girls are known for occasional hyperactivity and distraction, children who truly have Attention Deficit Hyperactivity Disorder face profoundly unique challenges at home and in the classroom. Kids with these disorders generally struggle in school and are often considered flighty, lazy and disorganised, labels that can lead to poor self-esteem. Because of a low tolerance for boredom and frustration, these children also frequently resort to mischief, leading to persistent discipline problems. Knowledge and understanding is a key to conquering the problem.

If you find out your child has ADHD, don't be in too big a rush to run out and make all sorts of changes. First, take some time to process your own feelings and reactions.

"Make me instinctively aware of the many strategies and procedures that can improve my child's behaviour, self-esteem and overall quality of life. Increase my understanding of ADHD. I want to provide consistency, sensitivity and structure. I seek specific consequences for their behaviour, and an organised environment where the demands are clearly identified ahead of time.

"Let me keep daily events like bedtime, meals, and homework on a definite schedule. Lots of rewards and praise for successful and appropriate behaviour are also especially important to happen. Let me accept them for what they are, my little darling child."

104

Cosmic Surgery

Doctors and surgeons could be more open-minded, and see beyond the symptom. Seeing the soul-spirit in every patient they take care of, the whole individual, not only the physical body and mind.

They would find that if they went beyond this boundary they would synchronise with the Cosmos and the Divine power that resides in every soul on this planet. The power that is within has the potency to change everything negative to positive, and it is at those moments that these doctors can do miracles with their patients.

If you knew the extraordinary Divine greatness and power you posses you would never have any difficulties or problems in your life whatsoever. This is not meant to be a replacement for conventional surgery, as at times, the two can and must work hand in hand. Always consult a doctor for medical advice. Perhaps while you await surgery you can try this Order.

"I believe I am worthy of allowing only good things to happen to me. Let my core being, my Soul, touch my spirit, and allow the Divine loving tool to enter me and heal me from within.

"I want to tap into this greatness of love and healing energy that will help to heal on the earth plane. I am healing, I am healable, I am going to be healed.

"Let the Divine energy that has received every healing thought, word and deed come to me and heal me. Allow my vibrational frequency within me be raised so as to communicate with that Divine healing energy, increasing my inner light and developing more love, compassion and joy in my life."

105

Detox my Body

Today's society lives in a time of technological development and advancement: computers, Internet, cell phones and new-fangled digital machinery that cause your body to be under stress. Add to this what is happening today as a result of the onslaught of chemicals in our foods and environment, and you will understand the need to detox.

Toxins block nutrients from getting into normal body cells. Oxygen and the body's food supply cannot get inside your cells to supply needed nutrients, nor can the cells' waste products get out. Diseases, such as cancer, now have an environment in which to form. When these body toxins are removed, your body can then restore a healthy balance.

"Remove toxins by cleansing my body. Restore nutrients. Let healing become a long-term reality. I learn more and more how to enjoy a chemical free diet. I am very good at reading my body. I am happy within myself, I will be happier at seeing nutrients restored, as appropriate.

"Let me taste the goodness of raw, healthy foods during mealtimes, at which times I will regain control over my diet.

"Water is the source of life, with every drop I drink I become more and more cleansed, as appropriate. Even though I am in control of my life, I will get more control over it.

"My faith and personal strength will allow a mind-approach that will be effective in making detoxification happen within me. Let all of this happen effortlessly from this time onwards."

Eating Disorders

The mirror screams, 'You're fat, you're ugly, you can't change'. Fixing your problem seemed easy at first - if you binged, you purged; if your body repulsed you, you exercised. But those 'solutions' drove you deeper into despair, self-loathing and addiction. Culture and its airbrushed perfection set an unattainable standard for most, whispering, 'If you're unhappy, do something about it'. Although the desire for change isn't inherently wrong, focusing entirely on body image can lead to obsession. Eating disorders offer a false sense of control, propelling you into a cycle of disease that robs your self-esteem, disrupts your daily life and affects your health, sometimes to the point of death. Only by escaping the trap and discovering the beauty inside can you find true contentment.

Numerous fashion and fitness magazines display impossibly thin models, setting unrealistic standards for young women. Startling statistics prove that eating disorders are often connected with this extreme pressure to be perfect.

One in three articles in teen girl magazines include a focus on appearance, and 50 percent of the advertisements use an appeal to beauty to sell their products. Twenty years ago, the average model weighed 8 percent less than the average woman; today's models weigh 23 percent less.

Approximately eight million women struggle with some form of an eating disorder.

A survey given by Harvard researchers to 543 fifth through to twelfth grade girls, indicates 67 percent of 'frequent fashion magazine readers' are more likely to diet or exercise to lose weight. Sixty-nine percent of the

107

girls said pictures in magazines influence their idea of an ideal body.

Over 50 percent of young women between the ages of 11 to 15 years old read fashion and beauty-related magazines.

Women's magazines have over 10 times more ads and articles promoting weight loss than men's magazines do, and over three-quarters of women's magazines include at least one message about how to achieve a better body.

It's obvious that the focus of the most fashion and fitness magazines is perfecting the outward appearance. Readers feel like they have to measure up, or measure down in this case, to look as good as the models. What they often do not realise is that the look they are trying to achieve is usually contrived.

"I want to be happy with myself, I want to be able to change at my own pace and for my own reasons. I have a desire to represent myself as a true version of how I am. I only need to live up to my image, I see my image as an image that is superior to the way others portray their image.

"The images I see in magazines and on the catwalk are contrived images, allow me to move away from that. Those images are fake and unobtainable to the average individual and, far and wide, the constant force of these images on society is wrong.

"Allow me to see the media-contrived standards for what they are: contrived. I do not wish to compete with an airbrush or computer generated image. I have the potential to be beautiful on the outside and the inside. I want my new standards to revolve around attainable qualities, including character, compassion, ability to love, obedience and much more."

Female Infertility

More and more couples are turning to fertility treatments to help them have a family. Female infertility is caused by some of the following factors: fallopian tube damage, endometriosis, male problems, etc. There is not sufficient scope to go in to all of these, but I hope that by invoking your Order that it will help to make your dream come true.

Sometimes there is more than one cause of infertility, you may suffer from endometriosis, but your partner may also have a low sperm count. The most common cause of infertility falls to the 'unexplained' diagnosis, which means that following thorough investigations, doctors can find no specific or identifiable medical problem at the root.

This particular Order is aimed at the female with the 'unexplained' diagnosis. Good luck!

"My diet is a healthy diet, let me enjoy an even healthier diet that is full of the essential vitamins and minerals that will correct hormone imbalances within me. I want to become knowledgeable about these imbalances, even more so than I am now.

"I avoid plastics and manmade fabrics even more than I do now, let me instinctively know what things to avoid. I only want to breathe in clean air, as appropriate, drink pure water and fruit juices. I can avoid caffeine with ease.

"My levels of the hormones oestrogen, progesterone, and testosterone will be monitored automatically within me so as to allow me to conceive naturally.

"I want my menstrual cycle to regulate itself so as to allow correct ovulation. Phasing of the cycle to coincide with the elements that allow me to become fertile."

Health Creation

How can you go out to work and support your family if you become ill after neglecting yourself? Don't you worry about the health of your children and immediate family? What if you are a top-flight sports star and want to avoid illness, what do you do to avoid coughs and sneezes that put you at your weakest? Perhaps you are already enduring ill-health and want to shake it off, or maybe you are sick of sabotaging your health and life expectancy with drugs, alcohol, cigarettes, overeating or lack of exercise?

Your best tactics in trying to avoid contagious viruses are to limit contact with infected people, and to avoid sharing personal items with them. Also, wash your hands frequently. A thorough, 20-second scrub with any soap and water will eliminate most germs. Keep your hands away from your face so the virus cannot enter your nose or mouth.

Whatever your reason for good health, make it your priority, even over wealth. Your health *is* your personal wealth.

"I want to use all the tools in my immune system to fight off illness. I want to start eating right and getting plenty of rest, as appropriate. Allow my immune system to act instinctively and to detect and destroy illness. I now want to live a healthier lifestyle and I ask that I am able to instinctively use my sixth sense to avoid illness.

"Let my immune system promote digestive health and improved immune function. Allow me to look out for those around me, and to help them avoid illness naturally. Ensure better health naturally for me in the winter and continually throughout the year, every year."

Male Infertility

A man will be considered at risk of being infertile if his sperm count is less than 20 million/mL of semen. The World Health Organisation defines this level, but it is important to realise that some men with low sperm counts (oligospermia) will still prove fertile whilst others with higher counts prove infertile. So a measure of sperm count is not a completely reliable method of assessing fertility.

If there are no sperm at all in the semen sample, the condition is termed azoospermia - there frequently is an ejaculate and a normal ejaculation process. Azoospermia occurs in about two percent of men in the general population. So whilst not common, there are plenty of infertile men around.

In addition, around 10-20 percent of men attending infertility centres will probably have azoospermia as well. Even rare is a condition known as aspermia - an absence of any ejaculate (semen). Retrograde ejaculation is a rare condition when some men ejaculate backwards into the bladder. This is a medical matter and will need surgery.

"My sperm motility will increase and produce good quality sperm. My sperm count will increase and I will be able to ensure my testicles are kept cool, as appropriate. The many biologic and environmental factors that can assist me will be invoked to do so. I want to become more active, less time sitting, and partake of sexual intercourse every fourth day. I will not find the need to masturbate.

"I ask that I can resist alcohol and drugs and remain calm within myself, allowing my GnRH hormone to be working on creating a high sperm count. I want to be accustomed to allowing my testicles to become used to ejaculating high sperm count semen."

111

Nightmare Control

Stressful things that happen during the day can turn dreams into nightmares. Nightmares may be a way to relieve the pressures of the day. Sometimes if you are sick, especially with a high fever, you may have nightmares. You aren't a baby if you feel afraid after a nightmare, as this is a normal reaction.

A nightmare is a very distressing dream which usually forces, at least, a partial awakening. The dreamer may feel any number of disturbing emotions in a nightmare, such as anger, guilt, sadness or depression, but the most common feelings are fear and anxiety.

Nightmare themes may vary widely from person to person, and from time to time for any one person. Probably the most common theme is being chased. Adults are commonly chased by an unknown male figure, whereas an animal or some fantasy figure commonly chases children. I must point out, this section does not deal with 'night terrors', as that is something quite different. Please consult a doctor for this.

"Let a normal psychic healing process start within me, nightmares will be diminished. My recovery is progressing well. I want the opportunity to dream normally and for self-exploration and understanding.

"I want to learn to decode the visual and symbolic language of the dream and to see relationships between the dream and waking life. I will become a more relaxed dreamer, and I want to do so by use of techniques that I instinctively have within me.

"From now on I want undisturbed, pleasant sleep, as appropriate. My dreams will become fascinating, creative acts of my mind."

Obsessive-Compulsive Disorder

Obsessive-Compulsive Disorder (OCD) is the obsession to do or not do a particular thing, or act in a certain way. This is a type of anxiety characterised by repetitive thoughts or impulses (the obsessions) and repetitive actions or rituals (the compulsions) that a person feels no control over.

Common obsessions are of being contaminated by germs, of repeated doubts and worries (such as excessively checking doors to see if they are locked), or of rigid rules for how things must be arranged. Some common compulsions are excessive washing of the hands, repeatedly checking doors or lights, or precisely arranging things in a particular order. The compulsive behaviour serves to reduce the internal anxiety felt by the obsessional thoughts, but usually lasts only temporarily.

"I want to regain control over Obsessive-Compulsive Disorder. I envision an electromagnetic force that is intensely healing, sent from the Universe, will neutralise my anxiety. Let it counteract recurring thoughts or images.

"I can let go of rituals, I am a strong enough person to do so. Let me become even stronger in managing this in a precise way. I want to undo obsessive thoughts.

"What I am asking for is realistic. I feel empowered by the Universe to make this happen. Let my thoughts be magical in their nature, yet logical for me to connect to the real world.

"Let my thoughts be free of superstition. My thoughts are harmless to me and anyone else. Let feeling and control be restored to my thinking. My confidence is increased, and symptoms are systematically eliminated."

Preparing for Surgery

Facing surgery can be a frightening and daunting experience that is fraught with questions, doubts, and uncertainties. However, most surgeries are elective, meaning that you decide if surgery is the best option for you and elect to have the procedure. This decision process often gives you needed time to prepare, which is an important step in using Cosmic Ordering in advance. Research suggests that those who prepare mentally and physically for surgery have fewer complications, less pain, and recover more quickly than those who don't prepare.

"I know I will relax while I am in the hospital and enjoy the attention I receive there. I want to be able to relax even more when I am there. I expect to have a painless and comfortable time before, during and after surgery.

"Allow my blood to be contained within my body as much as possible, and still be flowing and carrying repairing oxygen to all those parts needed. Let treatments and other medical procedures be of a painless and undisturbing nature.

"I have confidence in my doctors and medical staff, and in my own recuperative powers, I ask you to increase those powers. Assure that the surgical operation (or other procedure) will not shock my physical system or mental state.

"Each day I will continue to heal with good progress and become healthier than I already am in a natural way.

"See to it that I will not heed or be upset by any remarks or comments made during surgery, or negative remarks made at any other time, as appropriate."

Skin & Body Care

It's no secret that the human body is made up of up to 70 percent water. Muscle is made up of about 75 percent water. Fat is made up of about 50 percent water. Bones, too, are about 50 percent water.

The body needs between one and seven litres of water per day to avoid dehydration. The precise amount depends on the level of activity and the ambient temperature of the air, humidly and numerous other unfathomable situations. However, most experts agree that two litres of water per day is needed to maintain hydration. Drinking too much water can put you at risk from water intoxication, which can be fatal. Water benefits our skin by acting as an internal moisturiser, keeping the skin moist, supple, and clear as well as preventing premature ageing. Remember, by buying bottled water you will be adding to global warming, litter and solid waste.

"I enjoy optimal physical functioning, I want to enjoy that even more. My daily water intake is good, and is appropriate for what I do, ensure that continues.

"Let the healing molecules of that hydration add to my good health. Getting enough fluids will give me fresh skin, clear eyes and shining hair. I will enjoy regular daily treats of fruit and can derive benefits from sprinklings of salt, as and when required in my water, as appropriate. Let the salt reenergize me.

"Being near the seas and oceans of the world make me feel balanced, bathing in the sea brings me closer to the Universe and all within it, as does swimming in clean water. Give me the courage needed to do such a thing, take my shame away and allow me to bathe, swim or be near to the healing property of water."

Terminal Illness

Many people learn that they are suffering from a terminal or life-threatening illness from a doctor, at a stage when they may still feel only a little unwell and the idea that they may be going to die is completely unexpected. Most of us remain completely unprepared for our own deaths and the shock of having to confront it, particularly if you are younger, maybe with a dependent family, leads to turmoil of emotions and feelings.

Like bereavement, the first reaction is usually one of disbelief - the feeling that it is all some terrible dream. This is a very normal response for both the person who is ill and those closest to them and may last for several days or even longer.

The diagnosis of a terminal illness creates great feelings of powerlessness and lack of control. There are a number of positive steps that can be taken to help and support the terminally ill person and their carer, do explore them. They increase the feeling of taking control.

"Allow me to come to terms with what is happening, and to accept the feelings of those around me. Let the available resources that can assist me in coming to terms with my condition be accessible. I want to hold on to my mental faculties, have control up to my final feelings.

"I am willing to let my soul prepare for the meeting with the Divine entity and to furthermore allow those pathways to be opened up within from now onwards so that the Divine Light will direct me at the right time.

"Let my ether briefly remain after I have left my body so that I may console my loved ones. Allow ample time for me to say my goodbyes, let me touch those with love after I have left my body. I am ready to become One."

116

Bereavement Recovery

More than most, I am very familiar with this word. Even with all of my writing skills, I cannot do justice to describe the initial pain of losing a close loved one. Measuring my own personal losses against those I have worked with that have lost equally as much cannot be done.

I laid my mother to rest in May of 2006, within weeks of that I lost a very dear friend and then my ex-mother-in-law. Those in mourning surrounded me; they are the ones I felt so much for. Believe me, there is life after death, I assure you of that. There is just not enough space within this short piece to reveal what I know of this...please take my word for it. Be assured, your loved ones know when you are thinking of them.

"Ensure my loved one (name him/her) is taken to the higher spiritual plane, let them know I am able to cope. Let my loved one retain their astral body. Let it become refined as the lower sphere drops away.

"Let my loved one's soul have access to the Akashic Records (the Universe's super computer system) which records all events that have ever taken place anywhere in the Universe, as well as every thought and action of every individual. Let their soul review, in multi-dimensional sight and sound, significant episodes of the Earth incarnation recently completed. By reviewing the mistakes, personality faults and unkindnesses to others made whilst still on Earth, the various lessons still remaining unlearnt can be identified.

"Allow my loved one, if needed, to pass down spiritual strength to those on Earth who are lonely or in distress."

117

Beat Bullying

Bullying can mean doing or saying something that deliberately hurts, threatens or frightens someone: race, religion, weight, or sexuality, etc. Bullying is not normal, it does not have to be tolerated! Some people think bullying is a 'fact of life'. But bullying is wrong, and you don't have to put up with it. No one deserves to be bullied, whether that is in school, the workplace or home.

Bullying doesn't just come in the form of being ganged up on over a period of time; it could also be name calling, spreading malicious rumours, excluding someone from a group, damaging the victim's property, being heavily and continually criticised for your work, etc.

Silent phone calls or abusive texts or email can be just as distressing as being bullied face-to-face.

"Give me the strength to tell someone I trust to tell of this bullying so I/they can stop this bullying. I want to instinctively sense the places that are good for me and spend time at them. Give me the strength to stay calm and to walk away from negative situations. I want to act and be more confident than I am. I want to show others that I am confident.

"I am an open and receptive person, let me choose what I listen to at will, as appropriate. Allow my best judgement in remaining calm. I can control how calm I want to be. I want to be impervious to negative words.

"I know I can rely on my close friends, let those friends come to my assistance. I request them to come to my aid by my words of wanting to make it stop, let them.

"Let me be empowered so as to live my life hassle-free. Let me instinctively know how to sort out the situation I'm in or where to go if I need assistance."

Chakra Maintenance

Paying attention to the state of health of our chakra system will greatly enhance our health generally. We have seven primary energy centres in the human body known as chakras, although there are new chakras that are additional to these. Each chakra needs to be able to function at the correct frequency independently. Each needs to be balanced, clear, energised, and spinning properly. The chakras collect and direct energy in and around the body. Each time all the chakras reach a level of unison the entire physical vibration of the human body is raised.

Clearing chakras means flowing energy through chakras easily, regularly, and in the proper amount so that the physical matter will not deteriorate.

Healing chakras means taking active steps to resolve the issues that caused the blockage. You can clear your chakras over and over again, but if you do not deal with the onslaught of 'life junk' rushing toward them, they just get clogged again, just like spam hitting your email in-box.

Balancing chakras means regulating the flow of energy into the healed chakras so that it is harmoniously integrated into your being.

Aligning chakras means having balanced chakras working together in perfect harmony so that you experience vibrant physical, mental, and emotional health. Clearing and healing are about removing problems to become well. Balancing and aligning are about maintaining your state of wellness once it is achieved. The ultimate goal of chakra cleansing is clearing, healing, balancing, and aligning.

The Cosmic Ordering Service

So you will see why an 'out of tune' chakra can cause some problems within us. What I am going to do is give you an Order designed to keep your chakras at their optimum, but I would always recommend that you use some other form of clearing your chakras as a definite means to ensuring they are performing as they should. When placing this Order I would recommend that you lie down or sit in a relaxed and comfortable position. Your spine should be straight and your head in alignment with your body.

The first chakra is located at the base of the spine and is associated with the colour red. The second chakra is located in the area of the womb (or thereabouts for men) and is associated with the colour orange. The third chakra is located at the solar plexus and is associated with the colour gold (yellow). The fourth chakra (the middle chakra in the chain of seven) is the heart chakra and is associated with the colour green, and also the colour rose, which is the colour of love. The fifth chakra is located at the throat and is a bright blue. The sixth chakra is located at the third eye (mid-forehead) and is indigo (deep purply/blue). The seventh chakra is at the crown of the head, and is violet fading to white further away from the body. So here goes, a very long and worthwhile Order.

"I want my body to have good emotional balance, good physical health and good relationships with my surroundings and myself.

"I want to focus on the area at the base of the spine, the area between my legs, the root chakra. Let its energy be a powerful red, allow it to govern my physical body, my physical health and vitality. I want to mentally envision the chakra and note any symbolic symptoms and if my chakra is dusty, dirty, torn, or otherwise less than a

120

perfectly brilliant red whirling vortex, I want to work on that chakra. If it is dirty, let me clean away the dirt and throw it into an imaginary pail with a lid. Allow actions to repair any imperfections, and when the chakra is clean, I mentally take the pail and hurl it into the sun. Allow the sun to recycle this energy back into the Universe.

"I then turn my attention back to the root chakra. It is now clean and red. Let me be surrounded by infinite root energy. Let the room glow red, as appropriate, with this unseen energy, feel it's strength and power. As the energy swirls, let my chakra grow large, and deep red and strong.

"Allow the energy to fill my chakra until it is so vital that it extends several feet out from my body.

"Then I turn my focus up to my abdomen, to the area of the testicles/womb. This is the orange chakra that controls clear thinking and creativity. Allow those invisible hands to cleanse the chakra, to repair or heal it. Discard any imperfections in the pail, and send the pail to the sun to recycle the energy.

"Now I want to focus on the orange chakra again. It is now clean and whole, and a bright orange. Let the Universe hear my call for orange creative energy, let me feel the space around me begin to glow orange. With a tingle I will feel the energy begin to swirl into my chakra, charging it with vitality, with creativity, with clear-thought. Let me watch as my orange chakra grows and whirls, until it extends out from my body for several feet, just as the red root chakra is still whirling and strong.

"Now, I want to turn from the red chakra, up through the orange chakra, to the solar plexus. This is the heart of the yellow chakra that governs will and ambition. I want to take a few moments to examine this chakra. Let me examine my will through this chakra. Allow the invisible hands to cleanse the chakra and heal it, discarding any imperfections or impurities into the pail. Send the pail to the sun for recycling.

"Now I want to return my attention to the yellow chakra, that of will. It is now clean and a bright yellow. Universe, send me yellow energy, will energy, energy to achieve my goals, to work for that which I value and desire.

"Let me feel the yellow energy surrounding my body, and with a tingle, I will feel the energy swirl into my solar plexus. In my mind I can see my red/root chakra glowing, whirling, my orange/womb (testicle) chakra pulsing brilliantly, and my yellow/solar plexus chakra glowing strongly, extending several feet out from my body.

"Now I ask that attention can be turned to the middle of my chest, to the heart chakra, the green chakra. This chakra governs my feelings, my emotional connections to others and to the Universe, to life itself.

"Examine this chakra, gently allow those invisible hands to cleanse and purify the chakra. Release any tensions, imperfections or impurities to the pail. Send them to the sun for recycling. They are still mine if I choose to hold them, but for now, release any pain or anger.

"Now focus back on my heart chakra. It is clean, and a beautiful green colour. It whirls strongly and evenly. Universe, send me green energy for my heart! Open my heart to the world, to all beings, big and small, with compassion for our shared experiences and journey. Fill my heart with love energy, that I may in turn give love to others.

"I want to feel the green energy whirling into my heart, as appropriate. Let the chakra grow, glow and spin with this new energy. From the red chakra, through the orange chakra, through the yellow chakra, through the green chakra, my chakras are cleansed and charged and huge with energy.

"Now focus on the throat, centre of the blue chakra, which governs communication and personal magnetism.

"Now examine the chakra, noting the colour and any imperfections. Allow the hands to heal and cleanse the chakra and, when finished, send the impurities to the sun for recycling. Now the chakra is clean and strong and bright blue. I will feel the air fill with blue, Universal energy. I will feel my throat open, as appropriate, as this energy swirls into the throat chakra. This energy charges my aura with magnetism, drawing others to me. I feel my throat open with this swirling, strong blue energy.

"I now focus on the middle of my forehead, the third eye. This chakra is indigo and governs psychic vision and intuition. Examine the chakra for imperfections. Allow the hands to cleanse the chakra, to heal any imperfections and recycle them in the sun. Now I see the chakra, it is a beautiful deep indigo, clean and whirling.

"There is psychic energy available to me beyond measure. I feel it charge the air, swirl in and around and fill my third eye chakra with deep, vital indigo energy. I now feel the third eye open, and note any mental visions as this occurs. Let now be a good time to pray for increased psychic power. Note the red/root chakra, the orange/womb chakra, bright, strong, big!

"Now I ask you to move your attention up to the yellow/solar plexus chakra, to the green/heart chakra, open and brilliant, to the blue/throat chakra and the indigo/third eye chakra. Make my chakras huge, whirling, and fully charged.

"I now ask you to focus your attention at the crown of my head. This chakra is violet near the body, fading to white further away. This chakra governs my connection to the Universe. This chakra is like an umbilical cord to 'home'. Let me reflect on my spirituality of late, examine the chakra and allow any healing needed. Allow the hands to heal, to cleanse, and recycle the discarded energy in the sun. Now examine the chakra. It is brilliantly violet, glowing white around the outside.

"I now mentally reach out to the Universe. I will feel the response, the energy flowing back to me. I ask for the peace and joy of a strong crown chakra connection. I will feel the violet energy flowing in, a loving embrace of my whole Self, of my soul. I will see the crown chakra grow enormous, and the white energy surround my body.

"I ask that all my chakras are now clean, charged and in balance. From the red/root chakra, to the orange/womb chakra, to the yellow/solar plexus chakra, to the green/heart chakra, to the blue/throat chakra, to the deep purple/third eye, to the violet/crown, my chakras are spinning and whirling, full of energy and vitality. Let me see the white energy that extends up and out from the crown chakra, enveloping my whole body in an egg of white energy. I now want to be completely refreshed, calm, and peaceful. My energy is balanced. I will now be full of vitality."

Cosmic Ordering Hits a Brick Wall

You have successfully Ordered on numerous occasions, and then it suddenly stops and you hit the proverbial brick wall, what do you do? Stop placing your Orders.

There are many reasons why this has happened: deep-seated negativity has risen within you, you feel unworthy of your Order, you may have used 'dirty' language in the Order, made an ambiguous Order, placed an Order when not connected, unwisely demanded your Order, placed the Order on numerous occasions when connecting manually, placed the Order with insincerity, did not give specifics, has been some while since you last Ordered and you get it wrong, etc.

You either have a deep-seated negativity towards believing what will happen, and are therefore blocking your Order or you have some deep-seated trouble from your past that has been unleashed.

One question I usually ask of my Cosmic Friends stuck in this predicament is, 'How long ago is it that you cleansed your chakras? Please, don't answer...I bet you have never done this!'

I want to make one thing clear: I cannot personally help you cleanse your chakras, that falls to a different discipline, although you can use Cosmic Ordering to keep your chakras operating at their optimum. However, there is one problem! You will not be able to place an Order to help you cleanse your chakras, if they need cleansed! You will not get through to the Cosmos because of the 'squelch' that interrupts the connection. It's rather like saying your computer has crashed but you need to use it to connect to the Internet so you can download a programme to fix it! So until you cleanse your chakras (defrag your computer) don't place any Orders. There are various chakra-clearing books and audiobooks available on the Internet or via any good bookshop. The only one (to date) I personally recommend is by Doreen Virtue, it is called: 'Chakra Clearing: Awakening Your Spiritual Power to Know and Heal' (book and CD). I have to advise for the non-religious...the CD does contain some reference to religion, but it isn't something that you should allow to spoil the experience if you are not religious. I am currently working on a set of chakra cleansing cards aimed at Cosmic Ordering that will be available in 2007: 'Cosmic Ordering Chakra Cleansing: Oracle Cards'.

Once you have cleansed your chakras and feel up to it, this is the time to go back to placing your Orders. If you are certain that your chakras are in good working order then I would advise you to use 'clean' language and place a simple Order from one that is within this book. Then ensure you follow through with the advice I give you in my book 'Cosmic Ordering Guide'.

You have to consolidate your Order once it has been placed. Many of you are placing Orders and walking off into the sunset with nothing more than hope to help you along...this is not the way to do it. Remember, you must eat, breathe and sleep your Order...you have to want it to happen, believe it will happen and it will happen. If you have a shred of doubt or negativity then you will know in your heart of hearts that you are not worthy of your Order.

Negativity could be one of the main reasons why your Order has not come about, or there is just plain naivety. Don't think because you've read a few pages from a book about Cosmic Ordering that you know it all. Innocence is not the same as being naïve, as a child-like innocence can and does empower you beyond what you ever thought. Just look at a child waiting for Santa or the Tooth Fairy to make an appearance. Those were the days, eh?

Debt Crisis

Consumer borrowing in the UK has passed the £1 trillion mark. It is not only homeowners that face the prospect of paying off large amounts of debt. Students now graduate with a huge amount of personal debt. Evidence suggests that students may be deciding against higher education in an attempt to avoid beginning their working life with large amounts of debt.

The lives of people have been turned upside down by overwhelming debt. Most personal debt is built up through credit cards and personal loans, and fuelled by the increase in household utility bills, growing unemployment and the overhang from Christmas spending. The rampant buy-now-pay-later culture has reached new heights. So what do you do, default on your payments or place a Cosmic Order?

"Now is the time to take control of my debt. I can draw up a budget to see what I can spare to repay my debts. I want to be realistic and stay within my budget. Give me the fortitude to manage on my income, and give me the control to spend only on essential items. I want to manage on a set amount each week. I want to hold myself to managing on that budget.

"Allow me to have better control over ensuring utility bills are paid first. Let me switch to cheaper utility suppliers without effort. I am good at controlling my spending. I want to become even better at handling credit card use for essential items only. Give me the courage to cut store cards in half. I want to make use of what I already have.

"I want to change to a bank that gives me the best deal, I know I can find one. Make me win against debt."

Learning Ability

Intelligence is the ability to effectively adapt to the environment, either by changing oneself, changing the environment, or finding a new environment. However, there is no commonly accepted definition of what intelligence is exactly. Some believe that it is our ability to learn, others believe that it is our ability to adapt to the environment, and still others emphasise it as being our ability to cope with the environment and situations we are presented with.

In any case, intelligence is based upon cognitive processes, including perception, memory, reasoning, and problem-solving. Intelligence is not a cognitive or mental process, but is instead the combination of these processes that we use to adapt to our environment.

"My intelligence is not fixed, I want it to increase my abilities and my grasp of skills. Let me excel in situations I want to, while finding it easy to achieve learning.

"I want to make the most of my natural abilities. Consciously making use of my full range of intelligences. Allow more creativity and new ways of thinking to enter my mind. I want to excel at all seven groups of cognitive–contextual intelligence: physical, linguistic, mathematical/logical, visual/spatial, musical, inter-personal and intra-personal.

"Let the left hemisphere of my brain become even more superior in analytical function and language, and for the right hemisphere to become even more superior in visual and spatial skills, and to function more holistically.

"I want increased alertness and memory power. Let the mechanisms by which intellectual development occurs within me become more active."

128

Racism

I have first hand experience of this…yes, a white man living in England! You see, because my mother was German she was branded a Nazi. Strangers would approach her and call her 'Nazi'. I was bullied at junior school, at one point having to fight the whole school of 300 children in the playground during break time as I spotted a teacher looking on without intervention through a window! I promise you, that is the truth. That is what spurred me on to rip a wobbly metal sink pipe off the wall I was backed up to. I can tell you, I was like Braveheart! You should have seen them run as I chased after them. The end of playtime bell saved them. Never again did they dare say the 'N' word to me.

Yet, years later, my mother was adoptively called the 'German Geordie' by the very people that had given her the abuse and the 'Nazi' tag.

"Through my actions and behaviour let it show that I am blameless and that my self-esteem is high. Let the responsibility to protect me be enforced by the law of mankind. Let me speak up now and disallow the racism that is happening.

"Let my actions show that I am anti-racism, allow me to remain above those that stoop so low. Allow my alert actions to get across to others how it is affecting my well-being.

"I want to enjoy myself at home or with my friends, they will support me through it. Let me accept the kindness of others opposed to racism.

"I want justice to prevail. Let The Race Relations (Amendment) Act 2000 and The Race Relations Act 1976 strengthen my resolve to know I can win against racism."

Save the World

The phase of current change is now bringing rapid transformation to our world. A manmade tragedy is looming. There are billions of ways to save the earth from catastrophe, one for each living person. Everyone can be part of this global Order.

Mankind must make radical changes, changes that will come from new world leaders, not those currently in power. Once the 'new' breed of leader is in place then those radical changes WILL take place, we just need to accelerate their takeover of the planet.

You can help, your Cosmic Connection will make a difference, I can assure you of that. Let me show you how you can be of help. When I tell you of how the tiny phytoplankton in the seas act together as an enormous 'carbon sink' - their process of deriving energy from sunlight through photosynthesis converts masses of CO^2 into oxygen and carbon mass, which then sinks to the ocean bed, then you might get some idea of your might. You are far bigger and far more intelligent than phytoplankton, yet look at what they do.

As the ice melts and the water levels rise, it also warms and desalinates, altering the ecosystem that the fragile plankton rely upon to survive. As they disappear, so too does their ability to convert greenhouse gases into oxygen, thereby strengthening the greenhouse effect.

Between now and 2050, the world's energy needs are expected to double. A Climate Solutions document says technologies already available could be harnessed to produce enough sustainable energy to power the planet, while also reducing greenhouse gas emissions by 60-80 percent.

The finding is in stark contrast to the UK Government's insistence upon the need to go nuclear.

The current statesmen in power do not seem to have the radical courage needed, so it will take a great change to make it all come about to the way it should be.

Only when the last tree has died and the last river been poisoned and the last fish been caught will we realise we cannot eat money. Those that have transcended materialistic bounds are those that will be able to see the consequences of mankind's destruction. The only problem is you have to have the wealth to be able to transcend it. It is no good saying to the poor, 'Transcend wealth'.

This is why I want as many people as possible to secure the trappings of life, so that they can realise how important other things in life are. To date I have only come across two people that have secured Oneness, and both as a direct result of Cosmic Ordering themselves wealthy! So go for it, get rich and then start saving the world with the following Order.

"I want to save our world and to sustain the natural world through increasing awareness and caring for human beings and all other species, as well as inspiring and empowering people to change attitudes, habits and lifestyles - personally, locally, nationally and globally.

"I make my request to the highest Order. This is to value the continuation of life on Earth in its present form above all else. Allow a new movement in world politics to take over. Make those in power give supporting pledges in order to make such a commitment real.

"Let enlightenment of the world's peoples prompt them to assist in the saving of the world. I ask that the culture of materialism and enlightened self-interest be replaced by 'social and environmental' values.

131

The Cosmic Ordering Service

"I ask that the world may communicate via vibrational connection, the need that Mankind no longer apprehends the world as different from himself or herself. What is more, this understanding can be applied to living in the world and to tackling what is needed. From this point of view, the declaration to love and value life itself above all else applies equally to all experiences of life, both within and through the outer senses.

"Let the people conjoin as one with everyone and everything. Let the physical world be the basis of reality. Human beings would never do the things they are now doing to the earth if they thought they were doing all these things to themselves, let Earth become the focal point of attention and to receive the attention it deserves.

"Let there be a leap in global consciousness from identification with being a separate individual to that of being One with everything. By showing all what the world is coming to, make this change the behaviours of governments, business and private individuals and households to progressively derive the habits, attitudes, priorities and values that are needed to save the world.

"Avert climate change by changing behaviour. Show countries which try to take the minimum action to fulfil their obligations, or refuse to take part and try to undermine the actions of others see the error of their ways by how the climate is changing, as appropriate."

Transcending Challenges

Life always brings challenges to deal with. Struggle and strife have come as standard accessories with the package deal of this cruise. When those inevitable difficult moments come, you have a choice: instead of being swept away into an emotional flurry or numb depression, you can see such times with some objectivity.

Then, even if part of you goes into some agitation or sadness here or there, you can still be aware of the part of you that's witnessing all the play of your life - the still point of the turning world that exists inside of you. From that place, you can remind yourself that after every storm, there is a chance to awaken into a new golden sky and find colourful new rainbows to delight your heart, nourish your soul, and rouse your spirit.

"I always want to look for the positive in situations. Let it happen automatically for any situation at hand. I am an active participant in life. Empower my belief system to strengthen my outlook on reality. Let the seeds of a positive outlook that are within me create a more positive experience when I am faced with challenges.

"I want my thoughts to be so powerful that my viewpoint will manifest through and around me! Let a challenge bring out the best in me.

"I have the ability to have powerful portrayals in the way I can help other human beings. I have risen above and beyond a particular challenge in order to find value which benefits my life and which I can pass on to others.

"Let challenges be seen as opportunities for growth and transformation in healing my mind and body. My efforts will create the kind of life that's pleasant and fulfilling for me."

Addicted to Internet Porn, Cybersex

When it comes to surfing for smut, Britons top the lot, it seems. British towns claimed the top six spots in a global list of the places where the most people typed 'porn' into search engine Google. While many people may be able to dabble in Net porn with no ill effects, some run the risk of developing a serious, and potentially dangerous, addiction to online erotica.

Use of the Internet for games, gambling, messages, porn or cybersex can become as addictive as any other drug. Pornography becomes an obsessive relationship with fantasy objects. Because real people cannot compete with fantasy, pornography ultimately interferes with - and may even replace - genuine relationships. Cybersex involves online chat rooms and online sexual encounters, and generally includes several aspects of pornography.

"I want to admit my addiction, I want to develop healthier patterns of relating to the 'real' people in my life. I want to exercise complete abstinence from an online computer. Emotional and psychological factors in my life can now change for the better to make me stronger.

"I much prefer human contact over and above cyber contact, increase my control over this, as appropriate. I am strong willed, increase this will. I am regaining control over (name it, e.g., cybersex, etc); increase my ability to control this.

"I now want to get pleasure out of socialising with real people - my friends and family. I want to spend more time with those I love in the offline world.

"I will buy and upload software on to my computer that limits my access to such cyber sites. My persona is always real, I let go of the pretence. Let that happen now."

Addicted to Sex

Sexual addiction is hard for many people to take seriously, but for sufferers and their partners it can be devastating.

Experts define sexual addiction as any sexual activity that feels out of control. A sex addict feels compelled to seek out and engage in sexual behaviour, in spite of the problems it may cause in their personal, social and work lives.

Sexual addition can take many forms, but it's generally characterised by behaviour that feels out of control. This behaviour might include excessive use of pornography, compulsive masturbation, high-risk sex, multiple affairs, etc.

Sex can become addictive in a similar way to alcohol and illegal drugs. During sex, our bodies release a powerful cocktail of chemicals that make us feel good. Some people get addicted to these chemicals and become obsessed with getting their next fix - their next sexual high. As with other addictions, the body also gets used to these chemicals, so the sufferer needs increasing amounts of sex to achieve the same buzz.

"I want to tighten the grip and control of sex addiction. The primal pleasure circuits in my brain will no longer override the rational function of my brain's frontal cortex, which governs rational thoughts. I want to regain control over the physiological changes within me. No longer does my central nervous system react, as appropriate, to such stimulation, I want to control sexual triggers.

"My high hormone levels will decrease to normal. My physical sensitivity will return to normal. Chemical chain-reactions in my brain that create the extra desire will rest."

Accepting Homosexuality

Though homosexuality continues to gain cultural acceptance, many who consider themselves gay or experience homosexual tendencies feel puzzled and even apprehensive about their sexuality.

Perhaps you've struggled with same-sex attraction, making you wonder if you're gay. Maybe you've even sought to meet your needs for companionship and acceptance through a same-gender relationship. If so, realise that you do have a choice in the matter. You're not simply 'wired that way'. For those with unanswered questions or a desire to change, there is a compassionate message of transformation and truth.

Attraction to someone of the same sex does not brand you as a homosexual. Often same-sex attractions involve more emotional attachment than sexual chemistry. Perhaps you are drawn to the engaging kindness, generosity or affirmations of a person of your same sex.

"I find I am highly dependent on same-gender relationships to fill my void for validation and security. I want to learn to accept healthy same-sex demonstrations of love and acceptance of sexual overtures.

"I feel the need in satisfying emotional needs in a healthy way. My sexual feelings can be acted upon with ease, let that happen from now onwards. Show me how to instinctively see out the root issues of my sexual attractions.

"Sexual experimentation with someone of the same sex is something I can do with ease. I find that I am adjusting to my changing body and budding sexual feelings. I can reclaim my sexual wholeness with ease."

Become a Latin Lover

The expression 'Latin Lover' describes a man of passion. If your partner has ever said, 'The only time you touch me is when you want to have sex,' you are not paying attention to non-sexual touch. When there is a lot of non-sexual touch, it makes sexual touch more exciting and more desirable. Non-sexual touch can be rubbing her shoulders or feet as you watch a movie, resting your hand on his lap while driving, or holding hands.

Smelling good is sexy. When your partner smells good, it makes you want to get closer. When you are close, chemical reactions can happen and ignite a fire! Really! I am talking about pheromones, the chemical Viagra. People stop talking when they feel the other isn't listening. This is a major intimacy killer.

You can plan and be spontaneous too. Add some spice by dressing differently, putting on a wig, talking with an accent, or going somewhere on a whim. Fantasise and take your fun where you find it.

"Let every touch, kiss, evening out, time spent together with my partner be as good as the first time. I want to relearn what my partner likes, in and out of bed. When I take my lover out, let me choose a location I am familiar with and whose main feature is intimacy.

"With each kiss, let us both cherish it as the first step toward what will prove to be a special relationship and move forward to the next stage. Let me show both control and tenderness when making love to my lover. Let my kisses pave the way for what is to come.

"I want to use playful exploration all over them with my tongue, and to keep improvising and coming up with new things to bring them to orgasm."

Cheating Partner

Suspect your date, lover or your spouse of having an extramarital relationship? Here are some of the signs: loss of sex drive, defensiveness, excuses, phone hangs up when you answer or gifts you never expected.

Recall the type of person you once were when you first started seeing and dating your lover or your spouse. That 'person' you once were is the person whom your lover or spouse once loved deeply. Be that person.

Please do keep in mind that none of these signs are guarantees of a cheating partner. They are only indicators, and the more of them you see, the higher the chances something is going on. Save your relationship, here goes.

"I want to show my partner how I respect their choices more than anyone else's. I want to show him/her that I am willing to give them the freedom to make their own choices and respect his/her wishes. Let my partner feel more comfortable when being with me than with somebody else by virtue of how I give them unspoken choices.

"Already I avoid discussing issues relating to where he/she has been. I want to be able to become stronger within myself in letting my partner know through unspoken words that I know of what he/she does.

"Let my partner finds that he/she can breathe easier when being with me than with the other person. They will come back to me, with no effort on my part!

"Give me the strength to stop clinging to my spouse/lover like glue. Show my partner that I have become independent, carefree, and full of zest for life! This is the real 'me' whom my partner loves and likes to be with. Let this start happening from now onwards."

Children Being Used Against a Partner

Manipulating children to get information or give information, misuse or disrespect of visitation time, withholding child support payments, bribing children with gifts or activities, undermining the other parent's authority, blaming or putting down the other parent in front of the children, using subtle manipulation to brainwash the child into believing one parent is trying to prevent the child from seeing the other, competing to be the most caring parent in the child's eyes is another type of abuse.

Children growing up in single-parent families are twice as likely as their counterparts to develop serious psychiatric illnesses and addictions later in life, according to an important study that was covered in *The Lancet* medical journal.

Researchers have for years debated whether children from broken homes bounce back or whether they are more likely than kids whose parents stay together to develop serious emotional problems.

"Being a positive non-violent role model for my children (or child) is what I want to be. I want quality parenting to precede anything else, as currently appropriate, in the upbringing of my children.

"Let me show my children what emotional stability is, ensure they trust both parents. I want to show my children how easy it is to grow up intellectually, physically and emotionally strong by setting an example.

"The civilised values of culture are my beliefs, let these beliefs shine through for my children to see. Let me teach my children about a society that takes care of those in need so that they learn to understand a righteous path."

Increase Sex Drive

Lack of sex drive (libido) is common in women, but quite rare in men. In the UK, family planning clinics and Relate clinics see quite large numbers of women who complain of low libido. Many of these women have no problems with having orgasms. Rather, they have no real desire to have sex and their minds are not turned on by the prospect of lovemaking. Fortunately, for many women (and men) lack of libido is only temporary. They get over it by themselves, and are helped by expert medical or psychosexual advice.

It is always worthwhile investigating any underlying causes, as it may be a case that medical intervention is needed. Physical causes are hyperprolactinaemia anaemia, alcoholism, drug abuse, diabetes, post-baby coolness.

Contrary to myth, the menopause doesn't usually cause loss of libido, and many women feel a lot sexier and have more orgasms postmenopausal.

"Mind and body are always linked, let the natural chemical in my body called oxytocin that regulates other hormones and regular release be generated through satisfying sex and orgasm.

"Let my erogenous zones become sensitive to my partner's stimulation. My largest erogenous zone is my brain, turn my brain 'on' to allow my body's sexual desire for loving sex with my partner to increase.

"During sexual initiation allow increased blood flow to my sex organs, as appropriate.

"I want to approach my partner with an open heart and warm feelings, including forgiveness for any hurts or harsh words used in the past."

Love Rival in Your Way

Are you worried sick that you will never be able to find or keep your true love because of a rival? Do not do anything or say anything which forces your potential partner to do things or see things your way! If they have to make their choice whether they want you or the other person, give them no excuses to leave you for somebody else, show them your respect! No one likes to live under the control of another person.

Do not try to compete with your rival, if you have one around. When you are competing, you are struggling, and when you are struggling, you create a lot of negative energy around you, leading to unpleasant experiences with the people who just happen to be with you. Instead, try to create opportunities that lead to positive experiences, especially with your partner around. Let your partner feel that they can feel more at ease when he or she is together with you.

"Let my partner know through my respect for them that I value their decisions and choices. My actions show my (potential) partner that I am willing to give them their freedom to make choices. I respect their wishes.

"Through my own good ways and manners, let my partner feel more comfortable when being with me than with somebody else. All discussions I have with my partner are pleasant and unquestioning, let that win my partner/lover over to me.

"The type of person I once was when I first started seeing and dating my lover/spouse, that 'person' I once was *is* the person whom my lover/spouse once loved deeply. Let me be that 'person'."

141

Obsessive Ex is Stalking Me

In revenge cases, the Obsessive Ex wants the leaving partner to be punished or tormented. The Obsessor believes that the leaving partner deserves to be punished or harmed for perceived 'wrongs'. They don't love the ex-partner any more; the obsession has only to do with trying to wreak continuing damage to the ex-partner's life. They will even pursue avenues of revenge that harm their own children. So be careful.

Usually the Ex is seeking approval from you that he/she still has all the good things you saw in them. Sometimes he/she just needs to hear that they have qualities that make them worthy of another relationship. Of course, if they have been violent towards you when they were in a relationship with you then your safety is paramount...call the police at once. Do not try to reason with someone who is mentally unstable.

"Let me impart to him/her that he/she still has all those good things to give in a relationship and that he/she deserves someone who will appreciate that. Define who I am and what I want. Get me through the learning process that leads us to know ourselves well enough to choose a perfect partner.

"The qualities my Ex liked about me are qualities he/she can seek out in his/her next lady/man love. Let him/her know through my actions that people grow and that it would be right for them to move on now.

"Let them see by virtue of my words (written or spoken down a phone, etc) that they have what it takes to offer a new partner something good. He/she just needs reassurance, let my words impart that to them."

Power and Control (overcoming)

When someone will not allow anyone to make any decisions without his or her approval, then this really can eat away at your core. Now you can change that.

A control freak has to be there monitoring food consumed, money spent, utilities used (heat, air, water), phone calls, mail, time spent outside the home; governs activities inside the home; rules TV choices and volume; restricts right to decorate or organise home without his or her permission, refuses to allow repairs or replace broken appliances; controls clothing choices and hairstyles; will not allow the victim to express opinions or develop friendships; denies victim any free time to relax or recover from illness; leaves daily list of demands with a warning attached if they are not accomplished. Use this Order.

"Allow others to put their trust into my competence. Let others see me as unnerved in what I do. Make it easier than it already is for others to ask for my help.

"When those around me seek solace, let my Spirit within stabilise them. Make my identity and sense of well-being a source of calmness to others so as to allow them to release control tension without knowing it.

"I am in control of the situation, people will be able to relax in my company. Without people being consciously aware, let my voice show them they have a friend in me.

"My eyes are so powerful, the windows of my soul, let them beguile and disarm any control strategy around me. My breathing will remain regular when in such a situation as is needed, as appropriate. I remain calm and focused to those around me.

"Let me speak slowly, as appropriate, and deliberately. Let me be patient enough to listen carefully."

143

Relationship Breakdown

There are a variety of stages within a relationship, where in the initial stages the mixture of emotional excitement brought the couple together, and years later the love that emerges is very different.

Why do broken relationships hit us so hard? Part of the happiness in a close, loving relationship comes from being loved by the other person. Consider the parent-child relationship. Usually it is a two-way love relationship. If your father (or mother) dies, you know he didn't die because he stopped caring for you. He simply died, and you accept that. When a pet dies or even runs away, you realise it wasn't because your pet didn't care for you. But when a relationship breaks up, it's different. The love and care that once existed for you has dried up.

"A while ago I was a couple. The couple relationship is now gone. The activities I shared are gone. With all of those rituals gone I now want to feel the relationship is complete, it has ran its time. I no longer feel the interdependency I created. I now want my own hopes and dreams for the future. This person is not in my life, now I want to accept that I am single again, and to feel the independence of that situation.

"I want to reclaim my friends, now that I am single again. This will take place gradually as I experience the delight of those friends I want to click with. Let those friends that are loyal to me remain friends. Let the friends I had back when I was single remember me.

"I want my vision of the future to be clear of what I have gained. My thoughts and memories are good ones. Let normal functioning within me return from now onwards."

Sexual Fantasy

Fantasies are daydreams. Imaginary visions. Whimsical speculations. Wishful thinking. Everybody fantasises at some level. If you've ever imagined what you'd do if you won the lottery, you've used fantasy. Fantasy is a fundamental part of human nature.

A way of rekindling a waning relationship is by use of exploring sexual fantasy. There's a huge range of personal taste in sexual fantasy, just as there is in everything else. But many people feel uncomfortable with their own fantasies, fearing they're somehow weird if things that are unacceptable to others turn them on.

Imagining a partner in a sexual situation that turns us on should be encouraged, these fantasies are vital because they may express an aspect of our unconscious mind. For example, fantasies about being submissive or passive may be linked to a desire to experience high sexual arousal without personal responsibility.

"Sex generally starts in the brain. So let me have an active imagination prior to having sex. Therefore, with this, my sexual desire is heightened and arousal will be much quicker.

"I want an active fantasy life, let it add novelty to my sexual relationship. Let this be particularly helpful for my partner, let it allow them to become as sexually adventurous as I am.

"Let my imagination have free reign to experiment in bed, and to play out roles. I want to use this as a practice arena where I can build confidence before embarking on something new.

"Let my fantasy thoughts during sex make me refocus on sexual pleasure."

Wedding Day Bliss

Everyone wants his or her wedding to be perfect. Marrying the one you love is an amazing experience. You should share that happiness with all your family and friends, not just on the day but also throughout the planning and after your special day. Planning a wedding doesn't mean brides should feel pressured to succumb to monogrammed napkins, huge diamond rings, and complicated gift registries.

Wedding day superstitions have been around for as long as there have been weddings. Whether tying tin cans to the back of the 'getaway car' to ward off evil spirits or getting married when the second-hand is moving upward for good luck, many couples make superstitions an important part of their wedding day. With this Order you can make your wedding day bliss.

"I want to share all my wedding planning with my fiancé/fiancée, chief bridesmaid (or matron-of-honour) and the chief purse holder. Make the technical preparation and personal preparation be as I want it. I burn away stress by using gentle exercise. I am able to talk freely about the positive aspects of my wedding day, making everything positive. Even the best man can deliver his speech with complete confidence through good planning.

"I am able to delegate tasks to responsible people with ease. There are a lot of family, relatives and close friends around me who will only be too happy to assist me, let me be able to delegate and to ask them if I need to.

"I want to keep my sense of humour intact and simply enjoy the moment, let that be reflected in how I control things in a positive way. Let the ether around my wedding party cause all to enjoy the pleasure of the moment."

Attain Fame

This is something that is easier to obtain than you could imagine. The '15 minutes of fame' phrase was coined by Andy Warhol (1928–1987), generally acknowledged as one of the most influential artists of the twentieth century. Warhol was referring to the fleeting condition of celebrity that attracts media attention. However, be sure to grab your 15 minutes of fame and bathe in it, as the attention span of the public soon wanes and moves on to newer celebrities.

In 1968 Warhol made a statement: 'In the future, everyone will be world-famous for 15 minutes'. Then in 1979 Warhol reiterated: 'My prediction from the Sixties finally came true'.

"I have hidden talent within me, allow that to come out and to shine. I picture myself making more money in a day than most people do in a week. I want to be the best at something other people find interesting. I want to be radically different so that I grab attention from the media, in the right way and as appropriate.

"Let my instincts put me in the right place at the right time. Allow fame to come to me, let it happen naturally. I can find fame in one of many different genres, it could be through a scientific discovery, becoming a best-selling author, through sporting achievements, singing, acting, advising, teaching or anything I else I become good at.

"I can accept being idolised by adoring admirers and fans, let my talent be recognised as something special by virtue of what I achieve in my chosen profession.

"I may need the services of an agent or manager, let that happen and for me to be discovered by the media. I will work towards that goal from now on."

Immortality

Immortality is often portrayed in science fiction as fact! Although in reality, many believe it to be far-fetched fantasy. However, behind the scenes technological advancement in biotechnology, cryopreservation, nanotechnology and artificial intelligence, progress in life extension has already started.

Ian Pearson, head of the futurology unit at BT, told *The Observer*: 'If you draw the timelines, realistically by 2050 we would expect to be able to download your mind into a machine, so when you die it's not a major career problem'. When you consider he graduated in applied mathematics and theoretical physics, spending four years working in missile design and the past 20 years working in optical networks, broadband network evolution and cybernetics in BT's laboratories, then you have to take his prophecies seriously.

"Let my cell structure change to that of prolonged life. Fight illness and keep my mind active. Eternal existence comes about via the disembodied mind, the astral body, and resurrection. Let vehicles be used alone or in combination so that my human personality will continue to exist in some form after the death of the physical body.

"I want my astral body to have spatial entity which has physical characteristics such as shape, size, and spatial position. Let my mind be capable of continuing to exist and to function without the brain after the death of my body.

"Should my body be cryogenically stored and then thawed at a later date, ensure my cells escape damage. Let my disembodied mind be interested in returning to habitate my renewed body."

Slowing Time Down

The resonance of Earth has been 7.8Hz for thousands of years. Since 1980 it has risen to over 12Hz. This means that 16 hours now equate to a 24-hour day. Time is speeding up!

For those of you old enough, think back to when you were a child, how time dragged, how the long school holidays over the summer never seemed to come to an end, apart from in the last few days when time seemed to speed up. Now move forward to the present day, how time seems to fly and you never seem to have time to cram everything into the day! What if you could do something about the principles of time and be able to slow it down?

"I want to slow down time, speed, and the ever-accelerating pace of life. The self-accelerating system that makes itself go faster and faster and faster and faster will break down and stop.

"The natural environments, cultural infrastructure, ecosystems that I once never had time for, change my mistaken belief so that I now have time for these.

"I want to ditch fashion and commerce in favour of nature and culture, where time moves more slowly and powerfully. Make taking the long view once again natural and common, rather than difficult and rare.

"I want to practice patience, and learn how to slow down. In the realm of my spirit's awareness, time is slowed down to a crawl. Time slows almost to a standstill during that moment of thought. I want to slow time down in my consciousness.

"Let me see in my mind's eye and memory things slowing down, as appropriate. Time is the ultimate illusion. All time is in the mind. Make time collapse."

Cosmic Q & A

The questions that follow are actual questions asked of me by my Cosmic Friends, via email. For the sake of clarity some have been edited, as well as some of the answers.

Q When I listen to the audio CD, 'Cosmic Ordering Connection', I find your voice is so soothing that I find I am asleep within five minutes of track two. I have tried to listen to it at different times of the day, but I always fall asleep. I am therefore not even getting to the stage of connecting or placing my Order. Can you offer any tips or advice please?

A So long as you are not tired and sleepy prior to playing the CD you ARE connecting, you are just not remembering.

One way to know that you have connected is if you awaken naturally at the end of the CD. If you find that you have 'slept' on and on and awaken a good way after the CD ended (time it from when the CD starts) then this will show that you have not made the connection.

If you prove that you slept via the advice above then I advise the following:

- Do not drink coffee or alcohol for 24 hours prior to playing the CD.
- Get to bed early the night before and play the CD mid-morning the following day.

If you find that you are still 'nodding' off, even after applying this effort, then you may have early signs of a sleep disorder. Don't be alarmed! I am a partial insomniac...so no worries. You just have to accept that if that is the case then you may strike lucky and be able to react and interact with the CD every so often, just stick with it.

If you find that you are really sleeping then do look out for other signs of a sleeping disorder, as you may catch it early enough to be able to counter it quickly.

Q One of the things I have asked for is to be successful and get a distinction in my up-and-coming exams, which is very important to me and I'm actually feeling very sure I will achieve this now! My first exam is tomorrow so I've decided I will read the rest of your book after this. I'm also going to listen to the CD after that.

Anyway, the reason I write is because I'm a little concerned about why I am craving success. I am already successful for my age. I'm just 21 and will be starting a very good job, for which I will be well paid. I have not been particularly lucky in love, but have an amazing loving family and know deep inside that I'll find a man. But yet I still often feel unsatisfied. I get quite lonely and cannot appreciate that I'm lucky for what I have. I think it could be that I actually need more from life, even though I have done well.

Having said all of that, I'm not sure if I'm more telling you about the way I felt yesterday before I started reading your book because I am feeling very excited now! I have only asked for two things because I didn't want to ask for too much. I suppose what I want to know is, is this the right thing for me?

A Right, down to business. Already I have spotted another one of my 'supercharged' mind persons, you are one of them: easily bored, gliding through life, craving more and more excitement. You are in a group that is about 10 percent of the planet's population. You would make a great leader, rather like Richard Branson, as he is one of the supercharged minds.

You are so young, 21! Oh, la, la...your whole life ahead of you. You know, I have solicitor friends, and many of them tell me that they would rather have become something else: a GP, etc, etc. Now, in your case, you may well change occupation a number of times in your life, and all because you learn too quickly, you become bored with lectures, bored with learning and bored with those around you. You find new things fascinating, as with Cosmic Ordering...but how long before the book and CD find their way onto the back of the cupboard or are left to gather dust on the shelf? This is quite natural for you, so I am not offended by the thought of it.

You will flit back and forth to Cosmic Ordering over the years, this is fine, as it's just the way you are.

You need that 'umph!' factor to come into your life, so make sure your life partner (if you can stand being with someone that long) has the potential to constantly excite and ignite you. My dear Friend, how I feel for your loneliness, but you will still have plenty of good times, just try not to have that far away, 1,000 yard stare on your face when people are talking to you. Train yourself to look as if you are listening, you know what I mean. (See Order numbers: 4, 30, 35 & 40.)

Q I suffer from Obsessive-Compulsive Disorder (thankfully on the lower end of the scale). I have always, despite the problems OCD can cause, managed to study, work, have relationships and function as a 'normal' (what's that!) person.

153

BUT, here's the problem, my OCD causes me to have obsessional thoughts about another person dying. This person is very dear to me, and the idea of them dying is truly terrible. I have been having these thoughts for about ten years, and though they were (to put it mildly) not nice, I could live with them because I knew they were a product of my OCD. But now that I understand the power of attraction and that what we think about, I am so scared that my thoughts may become reality. In other words, my thoughts about this will cause it to happen.

Do you think that the Universe could interpret these genuinely unwanted thoughts as something which was desired? Or do you think that when these thoughts 'pop' into my head, and I immediately change them into a wish for long life and happiness for the person concerned, would this action override the first thought?

A Firstly, can I tell you this, you are more sane than I. Secondly, I do not subscribe to the law of attraction that you subscribe to…can the Jews be blamed for the Holocaust? Of course not. I am sorry, but this mumbo-jumbo is causing unrest amongst believers of TLOA. Can we be held responsible for the death of those we love and care for? Of course not! Can you be held responsible for 9/11 or 7/7? Of course not! The crux of your question is:

START
Do you think that the Universe could interpret these genuinely unwanted thoughts as something which was desired? Or do you think that when these thoughts 'pop' into my head, and I immediately change them into a wish for long life and happiness for the person concerned, would this action override the first thought?
END

Questions & Answers

Having an Anxiety Disorder doesn't mean you are crazy. It simply means you are experiencing higher than normal levels of fear or apprehension.

This sounds like panic disorder. What you have is a type of anxiety characterised by repetitive thoughts or impulses (the obsessions) and repetitive actions or rituals (the compulsions) that a person feels no control over.

Magic and superstition are as old as the human race. They have represented a way for us to try to explain the normally unexplainable, and to try to control the seemingly uncontrollable. They have therefore always held great allure and attraction. One might go as far as to say that there is a human tendency to think superstitiously. Just look, for example, at people playing their 'lucky' lottery numbers, or reading horoscopes to guide their lives. Clearly, OCD does not have a monopoly on such thinking.

There are limits, however. The average person can find a place for a little superstition without it taking over and causing them to be unable to function. Even members of primitive societies, where magic dominates most important decisions, can tolerate its presence without becoming paralysed

There is currently no scientific explanation as to why some individuals tend to have these particular symptoms, compared to any others. Many of those with OCD are constantly bombarded with very strange and doubtful thoughts about harm coming to themselves and/or others. Sufferers thus may feel that they cannot resort to ordinary protective measures, because of these extraordinary threats. Their world seems out of the range of normal control. They therefore turn to magic as the only other viable alternative, as a way of restoring a feeling of control.

155

The Cosmic Ordering Service

One other possible influence upon the development of magical thinking may be if an individual with OCD comes from a culture in which superstition plays a strong role. Coming from such a background cannot, of course, cause OCD. However, it can certainly help give someone at risk a push in the wrong direction if everyone at home is doing magical rituals.

Because sufferers identify words, numbers, actions, etc, as having magical power to cause harm or bad luck, the magical compulsions which are supposed to undo them are frequently seen to involve the same elements. These rituals are generally used to cancel out or negate the 'bad' magical elements by employing their opposites, such as thinking of health promoting words in response to thoughts concerning the names of illnesses.

In terms of what can be done to remedy magical obsessions and compulsions, I recommend a one-pronged approach of behavioural therapy. By behavioural therapy, I mean specifically, Exposure and Response Prevention. (See Order number: 73.)

Q I received your CD and I just played the track (with curtains closed) and placed my Order. During the session I saw in the place where my third eye is supposed to be situated a beautiful shape of an eye transforming into a smaller eye (sometimes it was a circle), beginning in black (may have been indigo, it was a very dark colour) then transforming into violet, towards purple. It was beautiful. I don't know whether this is a usual occurrence, which always happens when one closes the eyes during a meditation or that this is a special appearance?

Questions & Answers

A Regarding the colours you envisioned: white light includes all the colours, and black (the darkness) absorbs them all.

Our moods, behaviours, movements and desires are expressions of our soul guided by Spirit, and will find its expression in specific colours. Even the colour combinations in our clothes are nothing else but expressions of our soul.

The seven crystalline light bodies are different colours: Blue, Violet, White, Gold, Platinum, Ultra-Violet and the VOID one. Most ascended masters on this planet developed the blue, violet and white light bodies prior to their ascension. Through an unprecedented act of divine grace, human beings on this planet can now activate their DNA enough to bring in the Gold, Platinum, Ultra-Violet and VOID Crystalline Light Body for the first time ever on this planet.

What you experienced, my Friend, was all the colour rays of rainbow energy flowing down through your crown chakra. These rainbow colours are the red, orange, yellow, green, rose, blue, indigo, violet, silver, gold, white, and black rays. You experienced some of these colours. There is also ultra-red and ultra-violet. By stating your intent for healing, they will flow from the Universe to whatever level body you need them in. Do not be too concerned if you don't know how this works. Just by asking, it will happen.

As the rainbow rays flow into your crown chakra, visualise them entering your bloodstream through the arteries and permeating the cells of your entire body. This only takes a few moments to go from one end of your body to the other.

If you have a specific problem you wish to work on, you can ask for the colours to infuse that particular area of the body. The body listens to every thought you think, so just by stating what you want, it will happen. This thought/body connection is very important to know, because your every negative thought makes negative things occur, and every positive thought you have, takes the body to higher levels of consciousness. The worst problem is that we confuse our own bodies by asking it to do something positive and then doubting that it can happen. In this case, please refrain from doubting the positive outcome so you don't undo the good you have just done.

The colour violet has long been associated with spirituality. Having the highest frequency in the visible spectrum, violet is at the point of transition to the next octave of light. To the ancients, this transcendental colour was a spiritual rather than a physical phenomenon.

Diseases Treated with Violet:

Bladder trouble	Mental disorders
Bone growth	Neuralgia
Cerebro spinal	Nervous disorders
meningitis	Rheumatism
Concussion	Sciatica
Cramps	Scalp diseases
Epilepsy	Skin
Kidneys	Tumours
Leucoderma	

Violet is the colour of the crown chakra, which is concerned with the energy of the higher mind. It also affects the entire skeletal and nervous systems of the body. It is very antiseptic, purifying on both physical and spiritual levels. It helps balance the physical and the spiritual energies. Violet is effective in cancerous conditions of the body.

A violet light that leans more toward the blue shades can ease arthritis. Violet also helps the body assimilate nutrients and minerals. It is the colour of dignity, honour, self-respect, and hope. It is used to bolster self-esteem and counter feelings of hopelessness, as well as in the treatment of mental and nervous disorders. Its complement is yellow.

Precautions

May stagnate or suppress emotions - especially anger.

Purple is considered by many to be a high vibrational colour. It is this high vibration which gives it its ability for purification. It is effective to use when strong detoxifying of the body is needed, as in the case of cancerous or pre-cancerous conditions. Purple is purifying to the body. It can be used to stimulate venous activity in the body. It can also be used for headaches.

The red-purple range is beneficial to balancing the polarities of the body. The blue- purple range is effective in helping to shrink (such as tumours) and to cool, easing inflammations.

Caution/Precaution

Because of its high vibration, purple should be used sparingly. Too much purple can create or aggravate depression. It can stagnate or suppress emotions - especially anger.

Black is a protective colour. It is grounding and calming, especially to extremely sensitive individuals. It activates the magnetic or feminine energies of the body, thereby strengthening them.

Black is the spiritual colour for some religions; but it is the colour of death for others, although I do not fully subscribe to this, as black is my favourite colour! It promotes resistance, obstruction, opposition, and enmity. It wards off hatred and negative emotions.

Black is most effective when used in conjunction with white, balancing the polarities of the individual, especially in cases where the individual seems to be losing control. It can activate the subconscious mind which can put life and all of its craziness into proper perspective. It should rarely be used by itself, but always in combination with another colour. Precautions:

Black should be used sparingly, as too much black can cause depression or aggravate such emotional/mental conditions. Black also increases fear, suspicion and paranoia.

Q I had a fab vision of my future house during my connection and I also had a vision of a mini you hovering above my head, talking directly to my third eye!

Looking forward to listening again. Should I only listen when I am in medium to high vibration?

A You had an astral experience! I am pleased to say that you were really going for it and allowed your astral body to do the business.

Right now, everything you touch can turn into success. You are on the verge of enlightenment.

You ask if you should only listen to the CD when you are in medium to high vibration? Well, it sounds to me like you are quite advanced to be throwing that one at me. You will, obviously, know that by increasing your vibration that you can make a connection, but maybe not in the way you intended!

It would seem to me that you have some control over opening your chakras. Thus, you are able to raise your energetic vibration or life force energy to more easily connect with and communicate with those residing in spirit.

Personally, I would say that you should just enjoy the trip without trying too hard, allow me to do all of the work for you, let those chakras rest. Push on, you WILL become stronger.

Q I read a lot of books in English because in the Netherlands I find there is a lack of 'good' books (Dutch or translated) on topics as alternative medicine, healing and also on Cosmic Ordering. I've had some fantastic results in the past, but your book gives me a greater understanding of how it really works.

Because I value your professional opinion, I ask you the following question: I would like to work on developing my sixth sense, i.e. psychic abilities in order to become more successful in Cosmic Ordering. Can you recommend any books or methods on this topic?

A I do not have any books in mind regarding developing the sixth sense, as I managed to advance mine on my own. I can recommend you to watch nature, watch wild animals, birds and insects. See how they react, feel them, sense them. Soon you will start to feel as they do, put your Cosmic Order in so that you can increase this sense.

Q Truly, the Cosmos is an entity which is full of wonder and potential, and I can't get enough of learning about it.

The Cosmic Ordering Service

I have been using your Cosmic Connection CD for around five months now, and just recently I think I have developed the 'Sixth Sense' that you talk about in your book. I have enormous feelings of déjà vu; I often think about things, and they appear; I think about friends, and they phone me, etc. Something like this has happened EVERY DAY for the last fortnight.

One thing that has also happened is that once I am deeply relaxed, my whole body starts shaking, sometimes very violently. At first I found this disturbing, but find if I relax more instead of focusing on it, it gets even more violent! After this stops, my mind feels very clear; it is not an unpleasant feeling.

My question to you is, why do I shake? Am I receiving energy of some sort?

A Great, it shows that you do not have to be stuck in the heights of the Himalayas with a yogi or a mystic to experience such a shaking energy. Congratulations on cleansing your psyche of years of built-up 'rubbish'.

Sometimes the spine starts to shake and tremble after meditation. These tremors may last a couple of minutes, sometimes a bit longer, but never more than a quarter of an hour. For someone who is not acquainted with these convulsions, they might look like fits, but do not worry...they are not. Your system will be clean from the bottom up. It tries to heal the centre of the nervous system.

This shaking can also occur in the extremities of the body, like the hands or the feet, especially after meditation; a trembling of the muscles is caused by the destressing of nerves.

In the beginning, this trembling can be gross, but after a couple of weeks or months it slowly fades away.

This trembling is different from the very tensed one that old people suffer from. For in the latter case it is a sign of a *stressed* nervous system, while in the former case it is a symptom of a *destressing* nervous system.

What can also follow is what is sometimes called the 'Cosmic Joke', where you break out into fits of laughter...again, nothing to worry about, and you are not mad. Just let it happen. Your vibrational rate increases.

Meditation seems to strengthen the functioning of this parasympathetic nervous system, with the result that the body loses its tensions more rapidly and more fully. What normally, without meditation, is a rather slow process, is now greatly intensified. The effects of meditation on this nervous system are much deeper than the effects of sleep.

In the course of time these fits and symptoms grow more rare and their intensity lessens. Slowly they'll wither away. Your nervous system is by now becoming totally free of all impurities.

Psychologically, you are growing into a new man. Your capacity for concentration is greatly enhanced. You are an outpouring of creativeness. Your mind will become clear, as it has never been before. There is by now a great stillness in your heart. You will be at peace with yourself and with the world.

Because there is no blockade or damage in the nervous system anymore, *pranic* energies can flow without being obstructed or hindered. This gives a very energetic feeling in the body.

Q I really need your help. Last year my marriage broke up. Both my husband and myself had been suffering from depression. Mine had a physical cause - I have always needed to take medication to replace natural thyroid function. No doctor had ever told me that this would make me depressed, as well as having severe physical effects: lethargy, moodiness, overweight and sleep disturbance, amongst other things. My husband's depression was caused by job problems and I also suspect by some kind of post-traumatic stress as a result of a car accident. Miraculously, he walked away with just a broken sternum.

When he left it appeared he was having a relationship with the daughter of my former best friend. My friend knew about my suspicions and that my husband was planning to leave, but said nothing. Now I feel I have been doubly betrayed, by my husband AND my ex-friend.

In this situation it is very hard NOT to have constant negative thoughts, mostly anger against my husband and former friend, and feeling that I don't have a future. I have tried suicide but didn't take enough (pills) to kill me; they just made me ill for a few days.

Everyday I get up resolving to try and think positive, and almost every night I go to bed and cry myself to sleep because I've failed again. I just don't know how to break out of this cycle.

How can I use Cosmic Ordering to change my life and ideally get my husband back?

A I strongly advise that you do not proceed with Cosmic Ordering, not at this stage! You are badly in need of another type of help...perhaps counselling. Your broken relationship is going to need healing. I mean, *you* are going to need healing.

You are harbouring too much negativity, your subconscious is holding all that negativity. Yes, crying will help...cry until you can cry no more, I encourage that, as it will drain your pain.

Questions & Answers

Questions & Answers

Again, I do advise you to seek out some sort of help with what has happened. You will or may get worse before you hit rock bottom, and then the only way is up. I have had umpteen failed relationships, each one put me down! I fought back from each, and then went down again...and look at me now! Take stock from that.

Also, don't fall off the rails and find any old relationship, as you will just be using that as a quick fix. For now, stay away from any relationship, as it will probably fail. (See Orders: 90 & 96.)

Q I bought your CD and am very nervous to play it, because you mentioned about the sleep apnoea, etc. I do not believe I have sleep apnoea, but what happens to a person if one listens to the CD with sleep apnoea? What will happen, i.e. worst case scenario?

A Snoring is not just a recipe for marital discord; it can be life threatening, too, when a part of sleep apnoea. This disorder, in which breathing stops many times a night, can detonate dangerous cardiovascular stress. But scientists have long puzzled over why we should respond so fiercely to dips in the oxygen supply. Now a new study has identified the tissue and chemical changes that stir up the problem, a finding that could lead to novel drug treatments.

People with obstructive sleep apnoea cease breathing for about 15 seconds, every few minutes, hundreds of times a night. Besides feeling drowsy and exhausted the next day, people with sleep apnoea face high blood pressure and risk heart attacks and stroke.

Therefore, with this in mind, I would not like to be responsible for anyone with such a disorder to find themselves in trouble. (See Order: 38.)

The Cosmic Ordering Service

Q You advise not to try Cosmic Ordering if one is near to pylons, etc. I feel nervous as to what complications could arise?

A With regards pylons, you do not say how far away from them you are? I would advise a minimum of 100-meters distance from them before placing an Order.

Q Does Cosmic Ordering come with a set of 'commandments' as with any religious order? Are there do's and don'ts that we need to adhere to? I guess what I mean is, for example, if you swear really hard at someone or told a lie today, is that going to backfire on yourself tomorrow?

A I must say, I did have a little chuckle to myself when you raised the little matter of swearing! What I can tell you is this: all that is important is that you keep that chain of positivity moving by receiving good and then doing good; forget the dictum of religion, as Cosmic Ordering is not that. Some people would like to hijack it as a religion, but it is not! Anyone, religious or not, can partake of Cosmic Ordering. Anyone who is a liar or full of profanities can partake, as it will soon level you out as a person.

You will not find bad traits in those with Cosmic Ordering beliefs; you might at first and they might be tailing off, but they will eventually change to become good people. You do not need to follow religious dictum to become a good person. To work that one out, just look at how many religions have produced bad people.

Questions & Answers

Cosmic Ordering is all about indulging yourself and those around you; how many religions would endorse that? No, I do not want to be stuck in a Tibetan monastery, eating frugally for the next 20 years in order to find myself. Live life now, live by your own high morality; you know what you want, go get it.

Q I was wondering if things just 'naturally' will start to improve after I have listened to the Cosmic Connection CD, or if I should be doing something proactive to instigate change?

A You can be assured that there are positive changes going on within you. The minute the CD has finished playing is the time you should start to feel more positive. Most certainly, leave subtle reminders around the home of what your Order is. Imagery certainly helps, so do go big on this; your fridge is a great place to start adorning images of what you want.

Q Will I get an ego-boost by listening to the Cosmic Connection CD?

A The CD is not intended as an ego boost...this falls within an entirely different discipline and is not to be used as a means to boosting your self-esteem or ego. The CD cannot change your life by simply playing it, you have to want some change from within yourself, as this is then reflected in how your subconscious mind makes its Cosmic Order; you have no conscious control over this.

The minute you place your Order is the time things 'naturally' improve, even just by virtue of you feeling more positive.

The Cosmic Ordering Service

However! I do issue one caveat: do not use the CD if you are feeling depressed, as this will only compound that feeling.

Q Is there an age restriction on using the CD material? I told my 8-year-old about it and he was very curious and would be interested in trying it - is that advisable?

A Yes! Of course an 8-year-old can use the CD, in fact the child will already be closer to the Cosmos than you are as an adult. I would not advise using the child as a guinea pig for your own curiosity, as to entice a child to listen to it without any particular aim in their very young life is a waste and is not how the CD should be used. A child will only want what is within the bounds of their imagination and, as you know, children have or can have wild imaginations.

To some degree, some coaching would benefit the child before use of the CD. Let them hear it without headphones on, let them get used to the concept, as they may equate it with the Tooth Fairy or Santa Clause, and when things do not materialise for them they are going to feel badly let down, as Ordering is also a mind related thing.

But, by all means, little Johnny or Jenny can gain a lot if the CD is used correctly.

Q One thing I was curious about was in terms of relationships; how best is it to get a helping hand in drawing a specific person towards you, so as to get to know them better without it being anything against their will?

Questions & Answers

A You desire to make your intended man/woman fall in love with you or to specifically have them befriend you falls to another type of discipline. You are trying to control other people remotely, which is an entirely different subject, and not one I can fully go into in such a short email reply.

You want to exert an influence to make a person do something, which is quite different to how Cosmic Ordering can fulfil your desires. Most certainly, you can influence someone to respond to your bidding, but this is far more advanced that Cosmic Ordering.

The Cosmos does not have a warehouse whereby it can fulfil such an Order, as the acts you are requesting to happen are not tangible. There has to be some sort of tangible commodity that can be supplied or something you want to draw out of yourself or for yourself.

Some people do request love, and that is supplied in the shape of someone to love, which is, sad to say, a commodity. But you can bring about what you desire in a piecemeal fashion, bit by bit, as you will see.

Certainly, you can request for your OWN life to have changes within it, as this relates directly to you, but you are trying to remotely control the actions of others, namely a particular man/woman.

Here is something to ask the Cosmos for:

I am a radiant being, filled with light and love.
I love and accept myself exactly as I am.
I now express love to all those I meet.
I am a radiating centre of divine love.
Divine love is working through me now.
I bathe in the unconditional love of my Creator.
Love radiates from me at all times.

The Cosmic Ordering Service

I love myself completely.
Love comes to me easily and effortlessly.
I give and receive love easily and joyfully.
Others love me easily and joyfully.
I now feel loved and appreciated by my parents, my friends.
I express love freely.
As I give love, I am instantly supplied with more.
I radiate love to all persons and places and things.
People are just waiting to love me, and I allow them.
I breathe in universal love.
I attract loving, beautiful people into my life.
I always deserve love.
I am attracting loving relationships into my life.
I project love to everyone I meet.
I love and approve of myself.

When our ability to distinguish the reality of an experience is suspended, we more readily fantasise, have more constructive visualisations, and begin to believe that the synthetic images are actually real.

Meditation can be an open door to psychic experiences of many kinds and usually involves turning our attention inward to the mind itself, which emphasises mental activity invoking the guidance of a higher power.

Differentiating between prayer, which emphasises communication with a higher being, and meditation, which focuses on developing oneself, it is important to understand that such meditation can induce an altered state that will help you gain what you want. (See Orders: 27 & 40.)

Q I have yet to demonstrate that Cosmic Ordering works. I put the CD to the test by asking for two things that were entirely possible to happen. I have waited and waited, and no show.

What does this mean if something doesn't turn up by the delivery date? Does it mean I can't have it and should forget about it, or should I ask again? My inclination is to ask again, yet you say we should only ask once.

A Not fully knowing your circumstances or the simplicity or complexity of the Order, I am going to take a decision here, a decision that makes me come to the conclusion that you either have a deep-seated negativity towards believing what will happen, and are therefore blocking your Order, or you have some deep-seated trouble from your past.

How long ago is it that you cleansed your chakras? On the Internet, look up 'chakra cleansing', or look up a book by Doreen Virtue, it has a free CD with it.

Once you have cleansed your chakras and feel up to it, this is the time to go back to using the CD, and ask for the same Order as many times as you want. (See Orders: 79 & 80.)

Q How many times can I ask for the same Order?

A Via the CD you can ask as many times as you want for your Order, as this is what the CD was designed for. Via the manual method...only once.

Q I'm so worried about the amount of debt that I am in that I can't seem to completely relax and I don't think I am making a connection. I have asked the Cosmos to increase my business or to point me towards a way out of my situation. I am finding it difficult to be positive when

The Cosmic Ordering Service

I am on my own, as all I am doing is worrying about my debt. When I am with friends and family I come across as a positive, happy, helpful person which is the true me. When I'm alone all I'm doing is thinking about my problem. I am just wondering if you could give me some guidance?

A You have to make a decision: keep worrying about money and by so doing you hamper your own positivity, or you have to admit that your finances are in a mess and things can only get better.

I noticed that you are true to yourself when you are on your own, but then you put a façade over your problem when you are with others. The odd thing is, all these people probably sense that you are masking something, as they will have their sixth sense activated by your guardedness. So why not come out with it and admit that you are working on improving your situation? This in itself is an affirmation that works to settle you down, then you can concentrate on Ordering from the Cosmos.

In the state of mind you are in, I have to advise that you should stop Ordering, first you have to look in to yourself.

Just as you say, your email might have sounded a little jumbled, then so will it be of your Order(s); they will be jumbled too. Tainted with your deep-seated negativity. Although I can relate to this.

My guidance on this is not something I take lightly, but after deep consideration I feel it best that you come clean about your financial situation to those around you. Then you can truly concentrate on being yourself and placing an Order. (See Order: 81.)

Questions & Answers

Q I have requested the house of my dreams and all the houses that I have ever shown an interest in came on the market within a couple of months of each other, but I didn't have the funds with which to buy any of them. I next requested the funds and in the post I received several sample cheques for large amounts with my name on them from these prize-winning places, saying that I had won the first prizes (no one else had received any of these). So I think I am getting my messages through to the Cosmos but in a muddled way.

I have listened repeatedly to CDs on wealth and abundance and positive thinking, you name it and I have listened to it but still things seem to go wrong. It's almost like everyone around me gets the big inheritance or the windfall and I get passed by. What am I doing wrong?

A There was one thing from when you first contacted me that stuck out, and that was how you informed me that everyone around you seemed to have everything so easy. I would translate this as you not being happy with your lot, and yet by focusing on what others have got, well...it distracts you from your goals in life.

There are a few routes left for you, although you have listened to nearly all of the CDs relating to wealth that are on the market, and when this happens with no results then you must look within yourself and question what it could be.

Here is a part of an email from a Friend of mine; see what she says about how she changed her past negativity (name withheld):

START

The Cosmic Ordering Service

The way I see it - and I have learned this from you - is that Cosmic Ordering is not about testing the Cosmos but rather believing in it - having the faith that it will deliver.

Over the past couple of weeks, I have come to realise - through your guidance I might add - that - in the past - I have had a lot of negativity within me and emanating from me that has probably blocked some of my previous attempts at connecting to the Cosmos in a positive way.

Positive being the operative word. It's no good asking the Cosmos to deliver if you don't have the faith and belief that it is going to deliver. As I said in my previous email - I feel that I now get it and so from now on - instead of getting anxious that something hasn't happened overnight - I am learning:

1) To check whether I have asked in a positive way
2) To be patient and to believe that what I have asked for WILL arrive.

END

My Friend, should you still feel that you are not feeling right within yourself then I would finally advise that you go for NLP and reframe your mind. (See Order: 11.)

Q At the moment I am focusing on my 3 x major outcomes: financial abundance, health & vitality and selling skills based on scripts that I have written using examples from your book. Do you recommend 1 x script per CD session? Or, would you address all three in each session?

A I would still advise that you shelve the CD for now, as I believe you have a natural aptitude towards Cosmic

Ordering. If you use the CD then you will spoil some of the hard work you have already done.

Already you have stimulated your pineal gland, it is functioning on a different level and has been 'flexed'. By using the CD you will be taking the shortest possible route, but you will always have to use the CD, as your connection will not be one of your own making.

I only want what is best for you; often I have recommend the use of the CD to many of my Friends, but very rarely have I advocated the use of the manual connective technique over the lazy way to connect.

Firstly, focus on your continued good health, and that comes above anything else. I would advise that you go piecemeal on these Orders, first one and then the other, and then the last one. Address all in one Order, via a manual connection with the Cosmos. (See Orders: 9, 17, 70 & 85.)

Q One of my outcomes is to boost my earnings as a salesperson, as I run my own business. I have set a financial outcome for 90 days time. Rather than just focusing on this alone, I am visualising and requesting increased personal qualities within myself that I wish to feel increasing daily – e.g. enhanced motivation, high self-confidence, exceptional selling skills, etc. Is this approach right for Cosmic Ordering? It seems to me that by requesting things that will influence my performance, I am likely to achieve the end reward sooner?

A Yes, this is exactly right! I have always advocated that Orders are placed within the bounds of a person's capabilities. Also, the tools you are enhancing and fine honing are your means to gaining this wealth. A lot of Cosmic Orderers simply ask for sums of money, they never create the means to how this wealth will come along.

You are targeting the right personal attributes to help you gain extra income. You already have fantastically astute skills in what you do, your self-confidence is awesome and will improve with each and every day. Your selling skills are beyond expectation, and yet they will improve even more...get my drift. Enhance what you already have, put it to the Cosmos this way, and you can be assured of a positive response. Use clean language, drop any negative words like 'can't', 'poor', etc. Build on your platform that you already have. (See Orders: 16, 17, 30, 42, 79 & 85.)

Q What are your thoughts on using a vision or picture board to display visual images of desired or requested outcomes?

A Yes, use all the positive imagery that you can lay your hands on, even have it in your car, in your pocket, by your bed, and it will continue to keep those positive vibrations alive.

Q There are currently many areas of my life that need a change of direction and fortune. By Ordering one specific Order, does that mean I may receive it even if a different result would be better for me?

I am about to develop my flat to increase the size and value, and I planned to stay with a relative during the revamp. However, I have now got a bee in my bonnet about leaving my job, and acquiring a new job.

I want to meet new people, feel valued again and have some fun. I was going to make this Order along with one for an invitation to stay with someone for a cheap rent while my flat is converted. Am I as mad as I feel writing this? If I did Order these changes, would the higher powers ignore them if they felt they would be bad for me or send them anyway and let me take the consequences?

A The first obstacle we have is, your life is already in transition, and from one day to the next your circumstances are changing, which means your expectation is always shifting. In essence, when you place your specific Order it is fine for that time, but if your circumstances change enough then it means your expectation of that Order manifesting itself has also changed, probably even into a negative thought.

By focusing on that one Order, regardless of situations and circumstances, then that is the possible outcome for you. If during the course of your daily chores it becomes apparent that the Order you placed would not be in your best interests, then this can be rather like bolting the stable door after the horse has...you get my drift? So do be careful what you Order. And don't forget, Order within the bounds of your capabilities.

No! You are not mad for writing what you feel within you. I do not know how old you are, but I can advise that we have seven-year cycles where change is likely to happen. So, say you are 21, 28, 35, 42, etc, then you are likely to have changes at those points in your life, give or take a few months either side of each figure quoted. So if you are hitting one of those ages then there are spiritual changes, and your need to feel recognised and valued will grow with age, up to a certain point.

The Cosmic Ordering Service

It sounds like you feel that life is passing you by, especially as you want to be in the midst of the action, and who can blame you? Indulge yourself and be happy.

You ask that if you did Order these changes, then would the Cosmos ignore them if it felt they would be bad for you, or send them anyway and let you take the consequences? Well, my Friend, I had someone email me, and within the text they were complaining that things hadn't been going well for them, and they also complained that someone had ran into the back of their car! Of course, my reply was that I had a puncture to my vehicle's tyre that week and I could not expect the Cosmos to prevent that happening, and that I did not have a ring or protective armour around me.

Now, just as that is the case then so it is with what you ask. The Cosmos would not prevent a set of circumstances from happening just to save you enduring hardship. This is why I tell my Friends to be careful what they Order. (See Orders: 12, 30, 42, 43, 79 & 85.)

Q While listening to your CD and placing an Order - should I only concentrate on Ordering one thing? Should I place an Order only once and not repeatedly? Is asking for exciting opportunities and wonderful offers too vague for the Cosmos? Do I need to really nail down the specifics, even if I'm not sure what I truly want?

A Once you have placed your Order then that is it, simple as that. However, the CD has been designed so that you can place your Order over and over again without antagonising the Cosmos, but only use this method with the CD. Do be careful not to place the Order outside the scope of the Cosmos, as this can convolute things.

Questions & Answers

Asking for exciting and wonderful things is the right wording, this is clean language. For instance, you should not say: 'I'm having a dull and unexciting time, nothing wonderful ever happens, please make these things happen'.

To rephrase, you would say: 'My life is full of wonderful things and adventure. Let exciting things, as appropriate, continue to happen to me'.

Nailing down specifics is far better, but use clean language.

Q We live in the countryside, but when we had electric put in they put a telegraph pole (about 50 metres) outside our front door, with a transporter (box on the post) on it. Would this affect Cosmic Ordering?

A This distance for a telegraph pole electric supply will not cause you any problems.

Q I live within 100 metres of an electricity pylon, will it cause problems when I Order?

A Indeed it will! Do your Ordering some place else, away from such powerful electrical interferences.

Q My partner took his own life a few years ago, then I lost my friends (as I guess suicide is not a subject people feel comfortable with) so they just left me to deal with his death on my own. Then I lost my job (not too surprised about that, as all I did was go to the toilet and cry), and since then I have lost my health.

I am exhausted and very much alone. I feel like I am in a bad dream when a monster is running after me and I run but stay in the same spot, and although my mouth is open and I scream no sound comes out of my mouth. I have been completely ignored. I went to my doctor about the hair loss, but he just said to me that it is now easy to buy good wigs.

When my partner died, I was put on an 18 months waiting list to see a counsellor. When I finally saw one, I had three sessions and was then told that I would benefit from a different type of therapy and was again put on a waiting list (which was 12 months ago). I feel completely invisible. I am not being heard or seen. Soon I think I'll just disappear.

I am trying so hard to be positive, but at the moment it feels like lifting a mountain. I find it hard to concentrate when I meditate as I cough so much. I always thought that when loved and surrounded by good friends it is half the battle won. I just don't think I can do this on my own anymore.

What worries me also is the fact that, according to the law of attraction (I have read many books on the subject), I feel I must have attracted all this to myself. I feel so confused, as I truly want to think positive, but unless something positive happens to help me out of this quicksand I just don't know how I can think or be positive. (See Orders: 4, 9. 30, 31, 34, 35, 42, 67, 70, 77 & 79.)

A I disagree with the laws of attraction, especially when the dictum of it is that you have attracted all of the bad things. Do you think the Jews attracted the Holocaust during the war? Impossible, yet this motley lot actually believe it to be the case. What then of all the happy Jews gassed in the concentration camps? They never expected it to happen to them. Sorry to rattle on, but some people will give any excuse to wheedle out of why you are like the way you are.

You lost your life partner, how could anyone expect you to suddenly pull yourself together? The time is not right, I cannot speed it up, and you have to go through your own set procedure of allowing time to pass.

All that I do get from your situation is that you are carrying guilt, you even cough to stop yourself chanting, which is a subconscious move to go against yourself and punish yourself even more. Only you will know when you have punished yourself enough, and you know that it is the case.

Within the scope of this email I cannot counsel you, and you will know from my book that I do advise seeking out therapy before going on to Order if such a loss as yours has been endured. Please seek out this sort of therapy, even if you have to pay something towards it, as there are some benevolent therapists out there. Explain your financial situation, they are good-hearted people and will help.

Please, do not use Cosmic Ordering until you have a brighter outlook on life, as it will only put a thin veneer over the situation. (See Orders: 4, 30, 33, 35, 67 & 77.)

Q Please can you tell me whether or not I need to put in my own Orders if I listen to the CD and, if so, how do I go about it?

I have no problem with relaxing and opening the third eye, but don't know at which part of the CD I would put in my Orders or if, indeed, I have to. You say that you do it all for me on the CD, so what do you actually ask for?

A Within the CD I have added many things that you are not aware of. However, I do wish you to know that you

181

have already placed your Orders via your subconscious mind. I have made this possible on the CD.

Should you specifically wish to place an Order then you will know the right time and place on the CD, as after listening to it for some time you will go into sync with it, that is how simple it is. I could overly complicate it by talking about false negatives, etc, but that would only cause you to wonder what I am on about, and you do not need to worry about such technical detail.

Order and be happy. I do not ask for anything on the CD, it is your subconscious mind that is in an Alpha state that does all the asking, be assured of that.

Q The main problem that I have is trying to stay positive. I work as a plumber on a building site, and have done so for the last 12 years since leaving school. I love being a plumber and everything to do with the construction industry. You have said that knowledge is wealth and this is a view I strongly believe in.

The problem is the lads that I work with. From the foreman down to the apprentices, they are the most miserable group of sods I've ever worked with. They cannot come up with one positive in a day, let alone a week. This is affecting my outlook and me. What can I do to change it?

A Being a property developer, I know the feeling re some of the tradespeople in the construction industry, but you know what? I know that when I am doing my job, which could be any of half a dozen things, I am working towards my own goals, not those of the man next to me!

I might get, say, a plumber in for some work, and he might have a face like a bulldog chewing a wasp, but do I give a meg? No! But let me tell you something, deep down I do, as you do too. And I can tell you what works: kindness! I mean, do you think anyone has shown these men gratitude over the years? Probably not! Now I know in your position that you are tied into being with these miserable souls, you feel hemmed in and cornered like a rodent. Well, try showing them the hand of kindness. When tea break comes, go for broke and open the biscuit tin, ask them about what they do after work, etc.

I recall one guy, a great big strapping giant of man; he would always revert to crudeness and would be gruff towards his fellow workers. Anyway, I don't worry about that, as I've dealt with killers and psychopaths from all walks of life (during the course of my crime-writing days), so no one can pull out the pretend hard man act to worry me.

So there it was, dinnertime. I offered a greasy chip to this man, and he accepted. It was a little like David Attenborough sitting with those gorillas in that TV documentary that is now quite famous.

What I am saying is, that it takes someone to start the dialogue, they are not going to do it for you. I don't know how long you have worked with these men, but in time you will all know each other's little habits and so on.

The problem is, if you start becoming the joker then they do not take you seriously, and if you suddenly change then they may become suspicious of your motives, which is why I am always myself...outgoing and friendly.

When you do eventually go home and share your life with the most important person in it, discuss your ideas with her/him/them. Let her know your dreams and ambitions, allow the hundreds of ideas rattling around in your head to come out.

Usually in this case, if all else fails, you have to ditch negative minded people, but you cannot ditch work. You have to realise that you could be a one-off, a throwback to when men were creative, the rest of your workmates are just doing their time and waiting for the day they retire.

Remember, the ant that stores the golden grain lives with joy and dies with pain. Your fellow workmates have a potential great workmate in you. Oh, and you will never please all of the people all of the time.

Q This morning I played your CD for the first time. The last thing I really remember was where you say that you will count to five and how I will be in a state of relaxation five times more than I already am. After that, there was almost like a 'click' or 'something' that made me regain consciousness and I heard you say, 'I hope you enjoyed the trip...I am sure you will see the results...'

Does this mean that it has worked? Or have I missed important material on the disc?

A Well, indeed, you should be pleased that you are so susceptible to the CD, you are more than on your way to where you want to be, and to achieving your goals. Be assured, you have certainly not missed any important material, it hit the important part of your mind and you made your connection.

You can be assured that if you were taken down to the same state then you would be able to recall what you experienced. You are lucky, you found the key to the door in an instant. Push on, listen to the CD as many times as you want.

Questions & Answers

Q How long will it be before I can expect to see my manifestations from my Orders coming to fruition? I know that's like asking how long's a piece of string, but it would be really helpful to hear in general how long it is before people start seeing changes taking place. I got the feeling from reading your book that your manifestations happened quite rapidly. Any help re timeframes, etc, would be so welcomed?

A For myself, re timeframes, it took a lifetime before I discovered what really made the Universe tick...but that is not the answer you seek. You see, my Friend, it is the expectation from within that sets the clock ticking. Yes, you will feel incredible during your connective state, as there are many physiological and chemical changes taking place within you. The vibrational frequency you have been putting out will change, that is for sure. How soon this happens is rather like comparing one child's growth rate to another child of a similar age, each has their own time frame. Some grow fast and some grow slow.

So, with this in mind, the aim of the CD is to accelerate that metaphorical growth rate, and that is what should be happening. However! You have the answers within. What we have is a communication with energy; some may call that energy by another name. Turning our attention inward to the mind itself, which emphasises mental activity, invoking the guidance of a higher power.

You need to be able to anchor yourself whilst in this state, and I would advise to you to use this embedded command prior to listening to the CD. Just before playing the CD, and whilst in a relaxed state, say to yourself in your mind, 'I only wish to use that part of me that will connect with the Cosmos, all other matters can be put on hold for another time, until I am ready.'

Repeat this a number of times in your mind.

On the other hand, since I do not fully know the circumstances of your Order or situation in life, you've Ordered, you've expected, but nothing has happened! Can you recall what I wrote in the book about 'Ordering within the bounds of your capabilities'? Well, you aimed high, but you might have aimed so high that you were not able to secure your Order, which has to be secured piece by piece.

Obviously, if you do not have the means to buy, say, a £150,000 bungalow or villa out there in lovely Spain then you have to consider where to start. Look at it this way. If I were to place an Order for a palace worth, say, £10m and it didn't arrive then I would not be surprised. However, I would not hesitate to place an Order for a property worth the value of the villa I just mentioned, as it is within my capability.

You are, though, on the right path, as you could have Ordered cash to the value of £150,000, which obviously would not manifest itself on your doorstep overnight. Securing what you desire in seeking to secure a tangible object is the right way to get what you want, but to step from, say, a small apartment to your own privately owned villa has to be secured in a piecemeal fashion.

I don't know what deep-seated negative feelings are within you, if any? Firstly, my Friend, look into yourself. Did you honestly feel that the Order was a possibility? If so, how did you think it would come about?

You see, my Friend, your first step to securing the rewards of your desires is to become at peace with yourself, have an inner belief in your abilities to secure what you desire. I do not know fully the circumstances of your life, so it would be so difficult for me to analyse your situation. For instance, you might not be working, you might be on low income, you might have a steady job but a mountain of debt, or you could even be sitting on a pile of cash but not wanting to spend it.

After cleansing your chakras of negativity, that is where you must start. Within the scope of this email I cannot go into detail about inner cleansing, as it has to be tailored to fit your needs.

I would advise that you stop using the audio-CD. Once you have cleared any deep-seated negativity then I would advise that you go back to using the CD, as it would seem that all what you are doing is putting a veneer of 'feel good' over what is beneath. So yes, listening to the CD will make you feel good during and immediately afterwards…but not for the whole nine yards.

END OF Q & A

So there you have it! I hope you have gained something from this chapter, and from the book. So sorry there wasn't enough room to get any more in, as there are some fascinating questions, but they are just too long to be able to use here.

Acknowledgement

To all my Cosmic Friends, thank you for supporting me and being so nice. I do value your friendship, you are my reason for doing what I do, thank you.

Related website:
www.cosmicordering.net

Some Other Titles From Mirage Publishing

Cosmic Ordering Guide
Stephen Richards

Cosmic Ordering Connection
Stephen Richards

Cosmic Ordering: Oracle Wish Cards
Stephen Richards & Karen Whitelaw Smith

The Butterfly Experience: Inspiration For Change
Karen Whitelaw Smith

*Burnt: Surviving Against all the Odds – Beaten, Burnt and Left
for Dead. One Man's Inspiring Story of
His Survival After Losing His Legs*
Ian Colquhoun

Prospective titles

Cosmic Ordering Healing Oracle Cards – Stephen Richards
Cosmic Ordering Chakra Cleansing: Oracle Cards – Stephen
Richards
Occult: Dispatches From The Shadows - Jonathan Tapsell
Past Life Tourism - Barbara Ford-Hammond
*The Real Office: An Uncharacteristic Gesture of Magnanimity
by Management Supremo Hilary Wilson-Savage* - Hilary
Wilson-Savage
The Tumbler: Kassa (Košice) – Auschwitz – Sweden - Israel -
Azriel Feuerstein

Mirage Publishing Website:
www.miragepublishing.com

Submissions of Mind, Body & Spirit
manuscripts welcomed from new authors.